Write a Food Truck Business Plan in Ten Steps
Business Plan Sample and Template Included

Table of Contents

2

Acknowledgments

The drive and determination to write this short novel were in no small part due to my wonderful wife, Tishauna, kids, Cara, Katy, Maggie, and Paul Jr., stepson, Jayden, and parents.

About the Author

Paul Borosky, MBA., Doctoral Candidate, is the owner of Quality Business Plan, Tutor4Finance, World Traveler Updates, and FinanceHomeworkHelp.net. His time is mostly spent with his family, business plan writing, writing books, financial modeling, and cruising. Oh, so many cruises.

Paul's first run-in with finance was as a mortgage broker in the mid-1990s. His fascination with finance led to an MBA with numerous credits in different finance courses. Recently, he has created two finance curriculums for a local college and is considered a subject matter expert in finance.

Currently, Paul is completing his dissertation, writing business plans, tutoring finance to students the world over, and teaching finance for a local college. In the future, he intends to write extensively related to business plans, vacationing, strategic planning, corporate finance, and incorporating financial modeling into startup and expanding organizations.

Introduction

As a doctoral candidate, professional business consultant, and business plan writer, I am often asked by aspiring and seasoned entrepreneurs alike, "What is the first step for starting a Food Truck business (or expanding a current operation)?".

When I first started out as a business consultant, I would explain to my client their place in the entrepreneurial process. I then support this analysis with proven academic and practicing business theory, along with recommending specific steps to take to start or expand their Food Truck operations.

After going through this process time and time again with Food Truck entrepreneurs, it dawned on me that the first step I ALWAYS recommend is writing a business plan.

Unfortunately, most entrepreneurs do not know how to write a professionally polished and structured business plan. Hell, most owners don't know how to write any type of business plan at all. From this issue, I decided to write this book focused on a ten-step process for writing a well-structured Food Truck business plan.

The Food Truck business plan writing steps include all aspects of the business plan writing process, beginning with developing the executive summary to constructing a professional and polished funding request.

In each step, I introduce you to a different business plan section. I then explain in layman's terms what the section means, offer a Food Truck-specific business plan sample, and analyze the sample to help you understand the component. The objective of this detailed process is to ensure a full understanding of each section and segment, with the goal of you being able to write a professional Food Truck business plan for yourself by yourself!

IF you still need help writing your business plan, at the end of the book, I ALSO supply you with a professionally written sample Food Truck business plan AND a Food Truck business plan template for you to use. On a final note, to put the cherry on top, **I have conducted and included preliminary Food Truck market research for you** to use in your personalized plans!

In the end, I am supremely confident that this book, with the numerous tools and tips for business plan writing, will help you develop your coveted Food Truck business plan in a timely fashion.

Step 1 –Company Description Section

The company description section of a business plan should thoroughly explain, in a nutshell, what the firm will do, how the firm will do it, where it will conduct business, and specific strategies that may, or may not, be used through the course of operations.

This sounds like a lot of information for just one section. And yes, it definitely is. This section, just about, is the only one devoted to thoroughly describing the inner workings of the organization.

Food Truck Summary:

The leadoff batter for this section is the company summary. The purpose of the summary is to give the reader a broad understanding of the organization. To accomplish this feat, make sure to answer the questions: who, what, where, when, and how, in one or two paragraphs.

Business Plan Writing Tip:

When writing the company summary, try to keep the section's content to a paragraph or two. Keep in mind; a business plan is a tool used for documenting the proposed business. However, due to internal and external forces in its environment (new products, competitors, etc.), providing too many details may lead to a plan that needs continuous updating.

A better practice, at least when starting up a business, is to leave some wiggle room for changes. The best way to do this would be to keep the scope of writing broad. In other words, provide enough details so the reader understands the business, but not so many aspects that the plan needs updating more than once every six months.

Sample:

Food Truck Summary

ABC Food Truck will be a limited liability corporation located at 123 Broadway St. in Orlando, FL. The business owner(s) will be John Smith. Our American food-themed food truck will focus on popular American menu items such as hamburgers, hotdogs, and corndogs. As for a side menu items, we will provide hand-cut French fries, home-made chili, and baked beans. The drink selection will include Coca-Cola products.

To comply with local regulations, our food truck will use an established commercial kitchen for food prep. The geographic area of service will be approximately a 50-mile radius from Orlando, Florida. The hours of operation will depend on the venue, typically, evening hours and weekends.

Analysis:

The structure above succinctly shows the name of the Food Truck, the type of legal structure for the business, menu items offered, location, and hours of operation. In other words, who, what, where, when, and how. Further, the information is kept in two paragraphs. Short and sweet.

Competitive Advantages:

The competitive advantage for a business is what the firm will do better than other competitors. As with most sections of the business plan, this concept may be interpreted in a multitude of ways. To illustrate, a competitive advantage may include differentiated product offerings, prime location, or even an exceptional serving staff.

Business Plan Writing Tip:

Think about how your firm will be different from other competitors. Once you identify and can state the differentiating factor, or factors, then explain why this is important for the business or to the customers.

Sample:

Competitive Advantages

ABC Food Truck will have specific competitive advantages once our firm starts operations. First, our Food Truck will use local, farm-fresh organic produce and dairy products when possible. No other competitor in the area has committed to this business model. By doing this, not only will our organization support local farmers, but we will also be helping to protect the environment by using organic raw material.

Analysis:

When discussing this competitive advantage, make sure to explain, in detail, what the competitive advantage is and why it's essential. Also, be detailed but concise. On a final note, always touch on one or two competitive advantages, but no more. The business plan should show some differentiation, but the differentiation should not seem too far outside of the norm. In other words, there are proven food truck business models out there, use them, and differentiate from them, but don't differentiate too much.

Product / Service Description:

In the product/service description section, make sure to thoroughly explain the product or service the organization will offer. To illustrate, an owner may list menu items and contents in each dish served. A menu item could be an "American Cheeseburger" and ingredients described as lettuce, tomato, mayonnaise, and American cheese. By doing this, the readers will fully understand the product and ingredients.

Business Plan Writing Tip:

Try not to exceed four or five services or products. Granted, a business plan should be thorough in this section. However, always keep in mind, the business plan should be balanced as well. Try not to have one section outweigh, in word-content, all of the other categories in the business plan. If the product or service offerings exceed five or six items, include the rest in an appendix.

Sample:

Product Description

Hamburgers
All of our hamburgers will be 100% Angus beef. Toppings may include lettuce, tomatoes, pickles, onions, a wide selection of cheeses, and different sauces like mayonnaise, spicy mustard, and Thousand Island dressing.

Hotdogs:
For our hot dog menu, we focus on creative toppings like homemade chili, sauerkraut, Cheez whiz, ketchup, mustard, and bread and butter pickles.

Side items:
The side item selection will include hand-cut French fries, homemade chili, coleslaw, baked beans, and cornbread.

Beverages:
Our drink supplier will be Coca-Cola. From this, product selections will include Coca-Cola, Diet Coke, Sprite, power aid, and Mr. Pibb.

For a full menu selection, please review Appendix A.

Analysis:

I chose to identify broad categories for menu items like hamburgers, hot dogs, and side items. Under each subcategory, I briefly explained the possible toppings offered. The objective here is to help the reader understand menu offerings at this point in time. As the menu develops, then more detailed information could be presented in the product section of the plan.

Pricing Strategy:

The pricing strategy section in a business plan should explain the business owner's thoughts and ideas concerning how their prices compare to competitors. Popular pricing strategies may include low-cost leader, premium pricing, and the best value pricing approach.

The low-cost leader pricing approach is when products or services are priced slightly below local or regional competitors. An excellent example of a low-cost leader would be McDonald's.

As for premium pricing, this would be when the business owner charges higher prices than area competitors, such as Apple, Inc. Often times, higher prices are justified due to differentiated services or higher-quality components.

In my most humble of opinions, my favorite pricing strategy, by far, is the best value approach.   For this strategy, the management team will continually research the prices of comparable product items or services offered by competitors in the area. From this research, the company owner will then create a base price for each product or service using the averages of competitors in the area. Next, the organization will make price item adjustments based on the quality of the services or overall business reputation as compared to yours. The end objective is to have all of your products or services priced competitively.

Business Plan Writing Tip:

When selecting a pricing strategy, make sure to use a financial model. By using a financial model, a business owner can see the impact price changes may have on customer volume and net profits.

Pricing Strategy Example			
Item	Low Cost	Premium	Best Value
Number of Customers	100	50	75
Average Price	22.00	35.00	30.00
Total Revenues	2,200.00	1,750.00	2,250.00
COGS	770.00	612.50	787.50
Gross Profit	1,430.00	1,137.50	1,462.50

In the example above, there are three different pricing strategies: low-cost, premium, and best value. Based on the financial model created, it looks like the best value approach will net the business owner the highest profits, even though the sales price is lower than premium pricing.

Sample:

Pricing Strategy

Our pricing structure will be focused on the best value strategy. For this strategy, our management team will continually research prices of comparable food and drink menu items offered by local competitors in the area. From this research, we will create base menu item prices using the averages of competitors in the area. Next, our organization will make menu item price adjustments based on the quality of ingredients, the ambiance of the competitors' eateries, and overall menu selection as compared to ours. The end objective is to have all of our menu item prices competitively priced using the best value strategic model.

Analysis:

This sample shows the business owner embracing the best value strategic pricing approach. Also, it emphasizes a specific strategy for implementing its pricing practice. The result is a well thought out strategy, which addresses the pricing segment of a business plan, as well as, allows for understanding the thought process behind the strategic pricing action.

Business Models:

One of my favorite sections to write in any business plan is the business model section. This is because a business model can be just about any action or process that makes the organization money. From this, business model sections vary significantly between firms.

Popular sections in the business model category may include discussions about product or service quality, hours of operation, number of workers, customer experience, or even the business owner's philosophy with treating employees or suppliers.

Business Plan Writing Tip:

When writing about business models, make sure to first identify the business model. Then discuss how the business model will operate. By doing this, owners can show how different aspects of their firm will impact their profits and or benefit customers.

Sample:

Business Models

Operations:

Our operational structure will seek to achieve a quick-service Food Truck's speed of service while offering high-quality meals that would rival a traditional fast-food dining experience. As a customer approaches our food truck, they will be met with our menu posted on the truck or chalkboard stand out front. This will allow visitors to decide upon their favorite dish before approaching the order window.

At the order window, our customers will be able to point to and select food items for purchase. Once the selection process is complete, we cook the items and bring the food to the "pickup" window for payment. In total, the process for each guest should be less than three minutes.

Hours of Operations:

Our hours of operations business model will be structured to ensure our Food Truck customers' needs are met at a convenient time. From this, our organization will be open based on venue operating hours. For example, if a food truck rally is held from 4 PM to 8 PM, then our operating hours will reflect this timeframe.

Analysis:

The example above is based on a general Food Truck operation. Specifically, the perspective for the business model used was from the customer. By including the customer's perspective of operations, the owner can describe the customer's experience and show why the operational structure has been created to achieve the desired experience.

As for hours of operation, personally, I like to address this segment in the business model section, as well. The strategy is utilized simply to keep operational business components in one section.

Location:

The location section of the business plan will definitely be structured differently, depending on the industry. Usually, in the location section, I will first note the company's address. Once this is done, then a discussion about the inherent benefits of the location should be discussed. For example, make sure to discuss square footage, utilization of the square footage, and layout of the site. Once complete, next discuss the external benefits of the location. External benefits may include parking availability, proximity to your target market demographics, and distance from major thoroughfares.

Business Plan Writing Tip:

For most of my business plans, I prefer to include a map picture with the location address labeled. This helps to emphasize the external benefits of the location.

Sample:

Location

As previously stated, our location will be in the Orlando, Florida, area. The proposed location size of the food truck will be about 200 square feet. Approximately three-quarters of the area will be dedicated to cooking and prep operations. The rest of the area will be devoted to storage, equipment, and driving area.

As for competition, this area has few other American-themed food trucks within a several miles radius. This will enable us to capture a significant portion of market share in the area.

Analysis:

For my business plans, I like to label this subsection header in bold font. This helps the owner, or other readers, scan through the document and identify important pieces of information. Next, I always include the city and state, at a minimum, for the location. If a location or service area has not been decided upon, then the writer should outline the parameters needed for their food truck. For this example, the business needs approximately 200 ft.^{2} and the ability to divide the facility between the cooking and food prep operations and driving space.

Future Plans:

The future plan section should contain a discussion about the owner's thoughts and ideas for the future. The ideas may include expanding operations to new geographic locations or adding new product or service items. A popular discussion topic in this section is about starting a second or third company in a new region. Regardless of the firm's future plans, make sure to show a conceptual strategy for growth.

Business Plan Writing Tip:

My preference is to be rather ambiguous with future growth plans. For example, an owner may plan to open 4 or 5 new business locations within the next five years. In this situation, explain in your plan that the new business will expand to several new locations within this timeframe. This shows that there are growth expectations. However, a specific number of new operations are held back.

Sample:

Future Plans

Within the next 24 months, our firm will open new regions in the Central Florida and North Florida areas. The new food truck service areas and timeframe will be based on funding, leadership availability, and other factors. Further, our management team will introduce new menu items within the next 12 months. These menu items will be selected based on customer demand, how well the menu item will complement the current offering, and the availability of fresh ingredients.

Analysis:

Notice that a specific timeframe is stated. This allows the business owner to set a deadline for when the expansion should be completed. Next, if the future plans include expansion, identify the general area in which the new food truck(s) may operate. This helps to set specific parameters for geographic development. In this case, growing in the Central Florida and North Florida areas show the business owner is seeking to exploit brand recognition in a specific centralized location.

Business Objectives and Time Line:

Every business will have specific objectives they wish to achieve. To accomplish the coveted objectives, owners need to list the objectives and have specific deadlines for completion. What better way to categorize a list of objectives than to put them in a timeline?

By following this structure, not only will an owner will be able to identify the objectives they need to accomplish, but the timeframe and order in which the objectives should be conquered.

Business Plan Writing Tip:

For this section, I like to break up the timeline into three to six-month timeframes. Further, when writing this section, I almost always start by developing the last time slot first. If my business objectives and timeline will cover up to two years, then I would start with the two-year point and work to the present. By following this strategy, the business owner can make sure each business objective aligns with the others.

Sample:

Business Objectives and Time Line

1 - 3 Months
- Obtain investor funding
- Identify the food truck and negotiate a purchase agreement.
- Engage in buildout activities.
- Hire employees.
- Start the advertising campaign.
- Open for business.

3 - 6 Months
- Document critical business models in the standard operating procedures manual.
- Survey customers about the menu and service.
- Evaluate marketing strategy.
- Evaluate business models.

6 - 12 Months
- Implement optimized marketing strategies.
- Implement optimized business models.
- Evaluate survey results and prepare a plan of action based on results.
- Examine external environment for market opportunities.

Analysis:

In the example above, I staggered the time frames between three months to six-month sections. Also, the further out I went, timewise, the broader the timeframe. This is because almost all objectives past six months should be broad due to the continual fluctuation of market activities. In other words, stuff changes too much in business to have specific objectives past six months.

In contrast, for the first six months, try to be as specific as possible. As shown above, for the first three months, I have specific objectives listed in the order that they should be achieved. This helps the owner stay focused on a sequential set of tasks for the short-term.

Mission Statement:

The mission statement section of the business plan should succinctly describe what a company will do to earn their revenues. Some owners like to focus on customer service as a center of their mission statement. Others prefer discussing the quality of ingredients or raw material used. Regardless, the mission statement needs to convey the owner's philosophy or mindset related to operations or customer service.

Business Plan Writing Tip:

The mission statement should be short enough so employees and customers will remember it. For my business's mission statement, I chose to focus on helping small business owners achieve their objectives.

Sample:

Mission Statement

"Our Food Truck's mission is to provide trending American-style foods; hot, fresh, and fast."

Analysis:

The sample started with identifying the Food Truck's main offering, which is American-style meals. Next, the mission described how we expect customers to receive their menu items, which was fast, fresh, and hot. This shows that our organization is cognizant of the needs and wants of our prospective customers.

Vision Statement:

The vision statement for a business plan focuses on how an organization will look in the distant future. Organizations may take a few different approaches to writing a vision statement. In the first approach, the statement may include the number of employees at that point in time, the geographic area serviced by the business, or brand recognition for the company. In most instances, the timeframe is dated 3 to 5 years into the future.

A second method is to forgo a specific time frame and focus on an "impossible" vision. The impossible vision helps business owners and employees continually strive to meet exceedingly high expectations.

Business Plan Writing Tip:

Selecting the vision statement format is pretty much an owners' preference. If a specific timeframe is used, then the vision may need to be updated periodically. For an 'impossible' vision, this type of statement is, more or less, static.

Sample:

Vision Statement

"Deliver world-class trending American-style foods delights on a national arena."

Analysis:

For this vision statement, I chose the "impossible" vision route. What I mean by an impossible vision is that objectively speaking, there is very little chance that a Food Truck will accomplish the stated vision. However, from a motivational perspective, this overreaching vision will help keep the owner focused on expanding services to new areas.

Value Statement:

The value statement should highlight specific values the owner and employees embrace and practice on an unremitting basis. In this section, use bullet points to convey the values for the organization.

Business Plan Writing Tip:

This segment is pretty straightforward. Popular values may be honesty, high quality, technological innovation.

Sample:

Value Statement
- Honesty.
- Fair prices.
- High-quality dishes.
- Technical innovations

Analysis:

These values express the Food Truck owner's commitment to fairness and honest business practices. As a rule, try to keep the value statement short and to the point.

Keys to Success:

Most business plans finish off the company description section with a discussion about "Keys to Success." For this category, focus on the business owner's perspective as to critical actions for success. Common keys to success include customer service, employee equality, and innovation. Again, in this section, use either bullet points or a graphical representation.

Business Plan Writing Tip:

Use a bullet point representation in the section to succinctly show thoughts and ideas about the actions or concepts that the firm will embrace and is essential for its long-term success.

Sample:

Keys to Success
- Innovative marketing.
- Skilled workers.
- Optimize operations.
- Service customers changing wants.

Analysis:

In each section, the key to success focused on a different aspect of the business. Innovative marketing related to marketing actions, optimized operations to the Food Truck's operational business models, etc. In other words, all keys to success are not focused on one area of the firm, but a range of different aspects for the facility.

Step 2 – Target Market

The target market section of a business plan should concentrate on a specific demographic or group of people, with similar traits or characteristics that need or want the company's services. At least, this is the "textbook" definition of the target market.

When I have my client described their target market, I like to set a scene for the client. The scenario goes something like this:

"You see a person walking towards you. There is no doubt in your mind that this person will absolutely, 100%, unequivocally stop in your business. What does this person look like? Describe the person in as much detail as possible. "

Here are some helpful questions to answer.

- What does a person look like?
- Is the person male and female?
- Young or old?
- How are they dress? Blue-collar worker? Executive? Office worker?

Once a business owner can identify their primary target market, they are now ready to complete the primary target market segment of the business plan.

On a final note, keep in mind, just because a business has a narrow target market, it does not mean that this demographic will be their only customers. The organization very well may have a broad appeal to a multitude of demographics. However, every organization has a limited amount of resources they can dedicate to advertising. Because of the scarce resource, having a target market in mind who will best appeal to the organization's advertising dollars is definitely advisable.

Primary Target Market:

Most companies will have several demographics that appeal to their product or service offerings and chosen theme. However, almost always, there is one demographic or group of people, that will most definitely want the company's core product or service items. This demographic is the primary target market for the firm.

Business Plan Writing Tip:

Make sure to describe the primary target market in detail. Also, justify why this demographic was selected. Not only will this help you understand who the firm is targeting for their product or service items, but why this group was selected.

Sample:

Primary Target Market

Our primary target market will be young, blue color works. Specifically, parents between the ages of 25 to 35. This demographic was selected because of their propensity to enjoy American-style foods at community events and other gatherings.

Analysis:

The target market selected shows that the food truck will focus on customers between the age of 25 and 35. The age demographic indicates that the business will embrace actions that attract a younger generation. Also, by identifying blue-collar workers, this shows that the business may best appeal to individuals working moderately paying jobs.

Secondary Target Market:

The secondary target market should be written in a similar manner as the primary target market. Except, a separate demographic should be constructed. By following this process, the owner is showing that their facility will appeal to more than just one demographic. In other words, having a secondary target market indicates a broad appeal for business offerings.

Sample:

Secondary Target Market

As for the secondary target market, this will be children between the ages of 7 and 12. This demographic was selected because they tend to accompany parents to community events and other festivals.

Analysis:

This secondary demographic indicates that the company wants to appeal to children as well as their parents. Also, selecting this demographic indicates that the firm understands it needs to have a general appeal to both adults and children.

Target Market Growth Potential:

Target market growth is another key component that should be addressed in the target market section of the business plan. Target market growth potential is how much growth an entrepreneur expects in their target market. Usually, this is measured in percentages or actual growth estimate numbers.

Business Plan Writing Tip:

When writing the target market growth potential segment of the business plan, I like to, personally, including a little bit of math. For example, if the blue-collar segment of the city is approximately 250,000 people, and the growth rate in the city has been 1.3% annually, we can then multiply the 250,000 by 1.013. This would give us a population target market 253,250 people in the next 12 months. This process may also be utilized in the same manner for subsequent years as well.

Sample:

Target Market Growth Potential

Based on research from the website ABC, the current blue color work force in ABC City is 250,000 people. The U.S. Census Bureau has noted that the city's population increased by 1.3% annually over the last five years. Based on this factor, our Food Truck owner expects a similar growth rate for the next five years. From this, the target market formulation will be 253,250 within the next 12 months. In two years, our target market population will expand to 256,543 people.

Analysis:

The important take away in the segment is that the Food Truck owner's assumptions, which are the population growth rate and the number of blue-collar workers, are sourced. By showing where your information comes from, the entrepreneur is adding credibility to the assumptions. The math, obviously, stands for itself.

Step 3– Market Analysis

The market analysis section of the business plan should address and examine the external aspects of the organization. Common external aspects of business would include the business's industry, competitor review, and possibly a discussion about the economy and its potential effects on the industry as a whole.

Industry Overview:

Identify the main industry the business completes. Once the industry is identified, then try and determine if there are sub-industries, with enough data, that aligns with your business concept. With this done, now research and take notes about the statistics and trends, such as total industry sales, growth rates for the industry, and popular tends currently being exploited.

Business Plan Writing Tip:

Thoroughly describe the characteristics and trends in the industry. For example, common characteristics would be growth rates, the price range of the product or menu items, and new business themes like gastropubs or food halls.

Sample:

Food trucks would fall under the umbrella of the street vendors industry. The street vendor industry sells quick-service type options like ethnic foods, ice creams, coffees, and even memorabilia from a mobile-type location. Revenues for the street vendors industry, as a whole, should exceed $3.5 billion next year. In the last five years, industry experts have found that the annual growth rate was approximately 4%. However, in the next five years, the street vendor industry growth rate should slow to about 1.5%.

Analysis:

This example started with explaining the specific characteristics commonly displayed by competitors in the industry. Next, a brief revenue and growth discussion of the overall industry was offered. This then led to addressing the potential revenues for the subsection industry, as well as the potential growth rate for the future.

Industry Statistics:

Industry statistics may focus on a wide array of topics. A great way to start the statistic segment is just to do an internet search about the industry and create a list of resources. Once this is complete, start reading articles and taking notes about the industry and specific statistics.

In going through this process, not only will the business owner deepen their knowledge about the industry, but they will also be able to show, through writing, in-depth research was done on the topic.

Business Plan Writing Tip:

When writing this section, I prefer to utilize bullet points to show statistics about the industry.

Sample:

Statistics

- The street vendor industry is one of the few food service industries that are growing at an above-average growth rate.
- Food truck operators can change their menus to better meet the changing tastes of consumers as compared to traditional brick-and-mortar restaurants.
- Because of the popularity and growth of the industry, new rules and regulations from local and state legislators should be expected.

Analysis:

This example shows various statistics concerning the street vendor industry. As you can see, the structure utilized is a bullet point format. To take it a step further, make sure to utilize footnotes for citations. This will add credibility to your statistics section.

Threats, Trends, and Opportunities:

The trends, threats, and opportunity section are an excellent opportunity for the business owner to show how "in tune" they are with customer trends, and industry opportunities. When I write this section for clients, I usually like to equalize the information with an even number of threats, trends, and opportunities. This shows a well-balanced and researched section.

Business Plan Writing Tip:

Even though "opportunities" is listed last in the title, I often start this section by discussing opportunities in the marketplace first. Opportunities in an industry may be found in a multitude of ways. Some business owners survey potential customers to find out their needs. Other owners will network with regional or national competitors to identify industry opportunities. Regardless of how opportunities are identified, make sure to thoroughly explain your findings.

As for structure, I prefer to use paragraph form for addressing the threats, trends, and opportunities.

Sample:

Trends, Threats, and Opportunities

An important threat to the industry would be related to the overall economy. Currently, job growth and employment are at all-time-highs. From this, people have enough discretionary funds to afford to dine out. Unfortunately, in the event of an economic recession, as discretionary funds for people decrease, profits for the Food Truck industry may show a correlated effect.

As for an opportunity, casual dinners are increasingly selecting "mom and pop" Food Trucks over chain restaurants due to better service, limited time for purchasing menu items, and appealing menu selections. This allows for startup Food Trucks to enter the market place and gain a loyal following.

Finally, trends in the Food Truck industry may be found in technological innovations. Technological innovations may help Food Truck owners offer better-quality foods or enhanced service for premium prices.

Analysis:

Each topic, trend, threat, and opportunity were given equal attention. Also, thorough explanations were provided to support each finding.

Keys to Success:

The industry "keys to success" section will different as compared to the "keys to success" discussion found in the company description category. As noted in the company description, the keys to success were written based on the business owner's perspective of the business. In contrast, the industry section keys to success use research, and the perspective employed should be from the industry as a whole. In other words, what are most of your competitors doing, and doing well, to be successful in the industry?

Business Plan Writing Tip:

For this section, make sure to do research and take notes. When I write the keys to success section for the industry, I often review articles related to industry leaders. As I go through the articles, I will jot down notes related to actions they have taken to be successful. After I have gone through several articles, I then compare the notes intending to find commonalities.

Sample:

Keys to Success

To be successful in the Food Truck industry, competitors need to focus on hiring skilled employees. In other words, small businesses must employ and retain qualified and well-trained workers. Qualifications may not necessarily be in traditional schooling. However, experience with kitchen prep, serving, and driving are necessitated to ensure that a guest has a memorable visit to a Food Truck.

Analysis:

In this example, the keys to success were focused on a small business owner competing in the Street Vendor (Food Truck) industry. An important identification, based on industry research, was the need for skilled workers. With this as a foundation, a brief reflection as to why this fact was focused on was needed.

SWOT Analysis:

The SWOT analysis is a popular strategic tool used by owners to quickly and broadly identify different aspects of the company's internal and external environments. Unfortunately, most owners utilize the SWOT analysis incorrectly.

The SWOT analysis is broken up into four segments, which are strengths, weaknesses, opportunities, and threats. This is common knowledge for most small business owners. However, what most small business owners do not know is that the strengths and weaknesses are one category, and opportunities and threats are a second.

In the strength and weaknesses segment, the owner should focus on the internal aspects of their business. What are the company's strengths and weaknesses? For the opportunities and threats section, this is where the owner examines their external environment, seeking out opportunities and potential threats to the organization.

Business Plan Writing Tip:

Make sure to utilize a visually appealing format, bullet points, and always, always have at least twice as many strengths and opportunities as compared to weaknesses and threats.

Sample:

Strengths
- Management experience.
- Documented plans
- Themed Food Truck concept
- Training program

Weakness
- Startup Food Truck.
- Untested business location.

Opportunities
- Community involvement
- Appeal to a wide variety of clientele.
- Location
- Brand building

Threats
- Local competitors
- Susceptible to economic downturn.

Analysis:

The most important fact to identify is the strength and weakness section focused on the internal aspects of the Food Truck. Whereas opportunities and threats segments concentrated on the external environment.

Competitive Analysis:

The competitive analysis section is where the owner has an opportunity to examine and discuss local or regional competitors. This section may be as short as listing competitors' locations, their distance from the target facility, and a paragraph summarizing the competitors' strengths and weaknesses. Or, this segment may be a full-blown competitive analysis analyzing important segments of each competitors' operation. For most entrepreneurs, the former approach is often best.

Business Plan Writing Tip:

The competitive analysis section, in my most humble of opinions, should be short and sweet. The preferred structure that I use is to identify the competitor's name, address, hours of operation, and a website link. With this completed, I then analyze the competition from a customer's perspective. To do this, just review the competitor's website and Google/Facebook reviews. In following this structure, the owner can gain important perspectives as to how the competition operates and, potentially, their glaring strengths and weaknesses.

Sample:

XYZ Food Truck is a "mom and pop" Food Truck in the Orlando, Florida area. The Food Truck was founded in 1984 and prides itself on its changing menu selection. As for services, the food truck offers a limited menu, focused on lunch and dinner. Based on a Google search, customers have had mixed reviews. Most reviews seemed satisfied with the food quality and service. However, some past customers complained that the cleanliness of the kitchen was lacking.

Analysis:

The short paragraph above succinctly noted the name of the competitor, a brief background of the competitor, if available, and a short discussion related to how customers perceive the organization.

Step 4 – Organization and Management

The organization and management section should be used to discuss the business structure of the company, management team, and job responsibilities.

Management Summary:

In the management summary section, most owners will include a brief bio about the founder and the management team. When writing the bio, make sure to highlight the skills and experiences that are associated with the company or perspective industry.

Business Plan Writing Tip:

Some business owners like to believe that their business is all about them. And for a lot of small companies, it is. However, if you examine the egocentric concept from an investor perspective, if something happens to the owner, then the investor may lose their investment because the business would not be able to continue.

Because of this important issue, try to keep the bio section at a paragraph or less each for the founder and executive team. This is enough information to demonstrate experience and competence. But, not so much information that the business owner and management team become the star of the show as compared to the business.

Sample:

Owner Bio

John Smith, Sr., MBA., is the founder and CEO of ABC Food Truck. He has started and managed numerous successful small restaurant/food trucks over the last ten years. Food Trucks/restaurants started, and managed, includes a breakfast cafe, pretzel food truck, and 24-hour diner. For each business, he was responsible for all aspects of the organization, from marketing to strategic planning.

Analysis:

The brief bio first identifies the position and job title. Following this introduction, a brief discussion about experiences was made. This showed the owner has qualifications for the new Food Truck and has supporting experiences as well.

Job Responsibilities:

The job responsibilities section is mainly included to help the owner demonstrate an in-depth understanding of the business structure and document potential positions needed. Further, by discussing and identifying job responsibilities, the owner can alleviate future disagreements between the executive team members. This is done by explicitly stating job responsibilities for the business owner, executive team members, and hourly staff.

Business Plan Writing Tip:

For larger businesses, not all positions and job descriptions should be included. For example, a job responsibility section might list the executive team positions, chefs, kitchen help, servers, and host position. This indicates that the business owner has at least a basic knowledge of the different positions needed for the establishment.

Sample:

Job Positions and Responsibilities

CEO:
- Create and execute marketing strategies for business growth.
- Align business strategies with the vision statement.
- Negotiating contracts with vendors.
- Ensure legal compliance for the business.
- Continually examine the firm's external environment for new market opportunities.

General Manager:
- Control inventory to ensure optimal levels are attained.
- Manage day-to-day operations of the Food Truck.
- Interview and hire new employees.
- Assist in the onboarding process for new employees.

Window Attendant:
- Smile and greet customers as they approached the truck window.
- Explain menu items and ingredients.
- Collect payment for food.
- Prepare and deliver orders to the customer.
- Work with the kitchen team to ensure high-quality food products.

Food preparer:
- Prepare all menu items based on the ingredient list.
- Follow all handwashing and other sanitary policies and procedures.
- Prepare food item prep.
- Make all menu requests accurately and adjust to customer's preferences.

Analysis:

For each job position, make sure not to list more than four or five functions performed. This structure helps to limit too much discussion about any one job position. Further, by staying broad with the descriptions, the owner cannot reveal too much about their operational structure and strategies.

Step 5 – Organizational Chart

The organizational chart section is pretty much a visual representation of the job responsibility section. The objectives here are to show each business position within the company visually. Also, this structure helps to convey the chain of command for the proposed business.

Organizational Chart:

The organizational chart should visually show each position within the company as well as whom that position reports.

Business Plan Writing Tip:

The honest truth is that most people will not read the job responsibility section. However, when individuals, such as employees, come across graphs or charts, they tend to spend a little bit of time assessing the information. From this, a well-prepared organizational chart will visually educate folks about the different positions in the organization and the chain of command expected.

Sample:

Organizational Chart

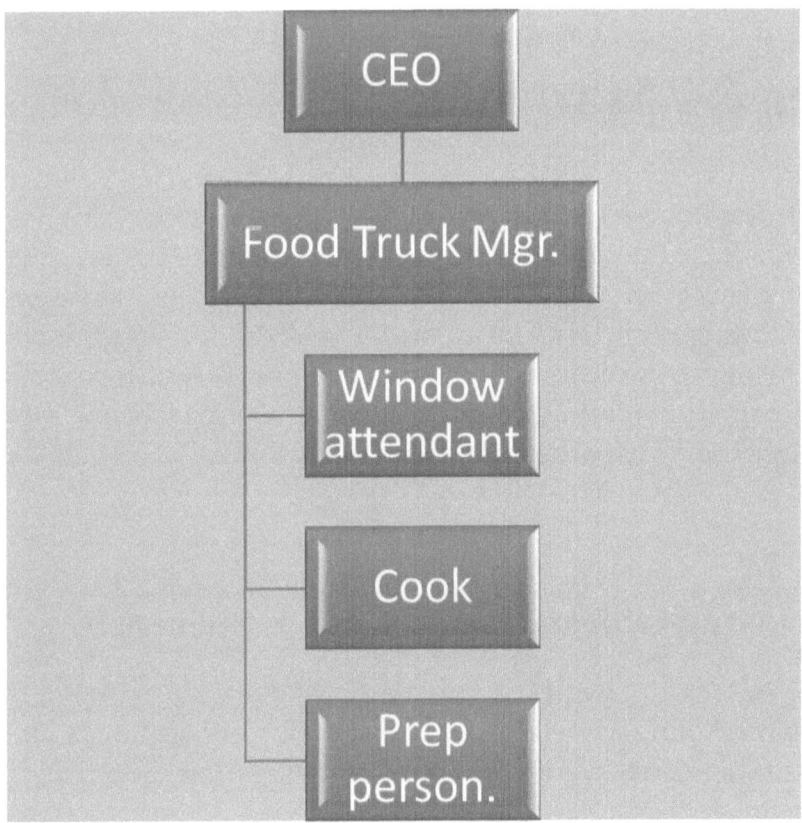

Analysis:

The chart above showed the CEO as the leader in the organization. The chain of command then moved to the food truck manager. The thorough example illustrated that the cook, prep person, and window attendant will answer to the food truck manager.

Step 6 – Marketing

In the marketing section, the owner has the opportunity to describe their thoughts and ideas about how the firm is going to connect with their target market. Popular forms of marketing may include social media, website, and traditional advertising opportunities. In most instances, business owners are going to exploit each one of the marketing channels to reach their target market on multiple platforms.

Marketing Objectives and Keys to Success:

In the marketing objectives and keys to success section, I like to use a visual representation showing the company's marketing objectives, as well as identifying specific actions that the owner needs to take to be successful.

Business Plan Writing Tip:

When writing this section, I always utilize a visual representation. This helps me convey, succinctly, my thoughts and ideas related to marketing and the objectives that need to be attained through the actions.

Sample:

Objectives

Market penetration.

Brand awareness.

Meet customers' changing needs.

Create marketing synergy

Keys to Success

Selecting appropriate marketing channels.

Continually keep customers engaged with our marketing material.

Periodically evaluate marketing actions for optimization.

Analysis:

In the marketing objectives section, popular objectives for Food Trucks may include market penetration, brand building, or educating customers concerning the menu items offered. As for keys to success, my preference is to focus on general actions needed to achieve their objectives. For example, if a firm selects the appropriate marketing channels, then the firm will achieve brand awareness.

Traditional Marketing:

Traditional marketing channels may include mailers, signage, and networking. Depending on your organization's location and theme, even your personality type, one or all of the traditional market opportunities, may be exploited.

Business Plan Writing Tip:

Make sure to list and discuss all your thoughts and ideas as to the different types of traditional marketing you may implement at some point in time. Just because you may not do mailers immediately, still address this in the business plan and, in general terms, discuss your thoughts and ideas concerning the topic.

Sample:

Traditional Marketing

Our first traditional marketing channel will include a professionally designed vehicle wrap for the Food Truck. This vehicle wrap will include our Food Truck name, logo, and slogan. Further, prominent colors will include black, gold, and white. The objective of the signage is to let potential customers know our Food Truck's theme and possible menu items offered.

Analysis:

In most parts of the business plan, I have a strong preference for being vague and using general descriptions. This is because entrepreneurs are, and should be, paranoid about competitors finding out their strategies. However, for advertising, once a marketing campaign hits, competitors are definitely going to know the strategic thoughts and ideas behind the marketing action. From this simple fact, in the business plan, go ahead and be detailed with your traditional in other types of marketing thoughts and ideas.

Internet Marketing:

Internet marketing is any type of marketing using the internet. Common Internet marketing actions may include developing a website, blogs, Google, or Bing paid advertising, and yelp postings.

Business Plan Writing Tip:

When writing about your Internet advertising, trying to touch on all aspects of Internet advertising that you wish to implement. For example, if you are going to have a website, make sure to talk about it, if you are going to register with Yelp or other business directories, then make sure to include this information in the business plan as well. By using this strategy, a business owner can show a broad understanding of potential internet marketing channels.

Sample:

Internet Marketing

The importance of a professionally designed website cannot be understated. To exploit this opportunity, the ABC Food Truck will create and maintain a website and Yelp listing. The objective of the strategy is to effectively communicate our Food Truck's theme and highlight our menu items.

Analysis:

I identified two specific Internet advertising channels that will be exploited. The channels are a business directory, which is Yelp, and the website. Further, the objectives of Internet advertising were discussed.

Social Media Marketing:

One of the hottest and most popular forms of advertising currently is social media. Social media advertising channels may include Facebook, Instagram, and Twitter. Because of social media's popularity, new channels are continually entering the market and trends with potential customers. From this, owners should not only explore and discuss using current social media channels but also review strategies to exploit new social media opportunities as well.

Business Plan Writing Tip:

A business owner may choose to discuss each social media advertising channel separately or go broad and outline strategic actions that may be employed in all social media channels.

Sample:

Social Media Marketing

ABC Food Truck's social media advertising will include Instagram, Twitter, and Facebook. Using a three-channel approach to social media will ensure our message reaches a broad audience, which will include our target market. Also, several potential customers will receive an advertising message on multiple social media outlets. This should exceed the needed repetition of our message to a broad audience as well as our target market. The marketing message will focus on our Food Truck menu items offered and possible weekly specials.

Analysis:

In the example above, our fictitious owner first introduced the different social media outlets the firm will employ. Once this was complete, the Food Truck owner explained, briefly, the strategy behind the social media actions. The final sentence touched on possible advertising content.

Step 7 – Financials

The financial statement section is probably the most difficult section for business owners to write. There are numerous reasons for this fact. First, financial statements are mostly made in Excel. Most business owners do not even have Excel on their computer, let alone know how to use the various functions needed to create financial statements.

Another common challenge with creating financial statements in Excel is the need to intertwine different pages. For example, when I create my financial statements, I often use one page, or tab, as an information page. The rest of the pages, located on different tabs, are tied into the information page using links and formulas. By doing this, if I change a financial figure on the information page, all of the financial statements are updated.

Financial Assumptions:

Regardless of how much time you spend on the financial statements, you will not be able to escape the simple fact that your financial statements will be wrong. I like to tell my clients that I have been writing business plans for more than ten years, and there is no way that I will know how many business plan appointments I will land tomorrow, let alone what my revenues will be in a year.

Because of this unknown, I create my financial statements based on expected revenues starting at day one. From this point, I will grow the revenues based on expected growth rates, which will be discussed in a bit.

To explain to the reader where the financial statement results came from, an assumption page is needed. The assumption page just tells the reader what your assumptions are for the financial statements. Common assumptions include daily sales and costs, monthly fixed costs, growth rates, tax rate, number of employees, and the cost of goods sold.

Business Plan Writing Tip:

When writing your financial assumptions page, make sure to explain any assumptions used in the financial statement calculations, starting with the top line of your income statement and ending with the bottom line of your balance sheet. For example, when I list my assumptions for clients, I usually start with the expected monthly growth estimates. From this point, I outline the expected cost of goods, the advertising budget, and so on. The objective of this outline is to establish credibility for your financial statements.

Sample:

Assumptions

Our financial projections have several assumptions based on research and management's expectation of potential sales and costs.

- All financial projections are based on management and or owner(s) professional expectations of sales and expenses for the foreseeable future.

- In the first 12 months, sales should increase by approximately 5% each month. In months 13 to 24, sales growth should slow to approximately .3% per month. For years three through five, sales are expected to grow by 4.5%.

- The cost of goods or variable costs are expected to be approximately 30.21% of total sales.

- The initial advertising budget will be $650. Advertising is projected to increase by approximately 1% per year. This is to ensure maximum utilization of the firm's property and equipment.

- Cost projections were calculated using a common size model. This practice is typical for financial modeling.

- The tax rate was assumed to be 20%. Fluctuation in the tax rate will have a direct impact on net profits.

- The initial funding needed is $150,000. An increase/decrease in amount will impact the net present value and internal rate of return.

- The starting cash balance needed is $28,300 for working capital.

- A cash account was used to balance assets with liabilities and equity.

Analysis:

In the example above, one of the first actions done was to educate and disclose the growth rate expected monthly for the first year. Further, the example went into more detail as to the reduction in the growth rate for the second year. By explaining the different growth rates, the business owner can show how financial sales were built.

The rest of the information just talked about various aspects of the financial statements, such as the cost of goods sold, starting a budget for advertising, tax rate, initial funding, and cash that will be in the bank once the doors open for working capital. This structure lays the foundation for the business owner to justify their financial statements.

Financial Summary:

The financial summary should explain the highlights related to financial projections. These highlights include revenues and profits for the first year, expected profits for years two and five, and, when seeking funds from an investor, possibly the expected return on equity.

Business Plan Writing Tip:

When writing the financial summary section, first start off by explaining that the financial section of your business plan is based on research and observations. This disclaimer helps to set the stage for the reader's understanding that the projections are just the business owner's best guesses. Next, follow-up the statement with your findings from your financial analysis. These findings should include revenues for the first year, net profits, and the profit margin expected.

Sample:

Financial Summary

The financial projections are based on market research and empirical examination of the local Food Truck industry. For the next year, we project revenues of approximately $423,976. The estimated expense costs will be $269,945. After taxes, we estimate a net profit of $116,074. This leads to a profit margin of approximately 27.38%. As our brand continues to grow, second-year progression is anticipated to yield a net income of approximately $156,299. Within five years, net income should exceed $178,980.

Analysis:

In this example, the organization expected first-year revenues to exceed $423,976. Further, the cost involved in attaining these revenues were also shown. This helps the reader understand the potential revenue generation opportunities for the Food Truck and the needed cost to achieve the dollar amount noted. Other important aspects of the summary would include the net profits for years two and five.

Startup/Expansion Costs:

The startup cost section of the business plan should include the costs needed to start the business. If the business is already established, then this segment should outline expansion costs. If funding is being sought and the money will be used for purposes other than startup or expansion, then make sure to use this section to reflect how the money will be spent. An example of this would be if a company needs funds to spend on an advertising campaign, then use the section to break down the costs for the campaign implementation.

Sample:

Startup Costs	
Category	**Estimate**
Equity Investment	20,000.00
Loan	130,000.00
Initial Build Out	75,000
Working Capital	28,300.00
Cooking Equipment	25,000.00
Inventory	7,500.00
Supplies	2,500.00
Training	3,000.00
Office Equipment	1,200.00
Misc.	5,000.00
Misc. Licenses	2,500.00
Total	**150,000.00**

Analysis:

When I set up my startup costs section, the first segment is always related to how much money the Food Truck owner has invested, funds needed from an investor, desired loan amount, if a loan is needed, initial buildout, and working capital, which are funds used for operations when the business opens.

It may be considered a little unorthodox to include funding with startup costs. However, by following this structure, the Food Truck owner succinctly showed funding needed and how the funds will be spent.

The rest of the sections focused on specific costs needed to start the Food Truck. The specific categories used were equipment, inventory, office equipment, and miscellaneous. In these categories, I strongly suggest that the cost estimates be inflated a bit. Say by 10 to 20 percent. Further, try to stay "general" with startup costs. This strategy is recommended simply because there is no way to know what your actual startup costs will be until your startup process has commenced.

Daily Revenues:

For my daily revenues, I always start with estimating revenues and the cost of goods for the first day of business. Revenues are the sales price multiplied by the actual number of menu items sold. For the cost of goods, this is considered the dollar amount that the organization spent to make the product or service. For simplicity's sake, I always utilize a percent for the cost of goods. This helps to stay true to using averages in the financial statements.

Business Plan Writing Tip:

When designing the average daily sales segment, always use averages for everything. By embracing the concept of using averages in the financial statements, the business owner is acknowledging that the estimates provided in the financial statements are the best guess approximate as to what the business owner hopes to sell in the future.

Sample:

Revenue Generators

Daily Sales	% Sales	Num.	Price	Cost	Profit	Total Rev.	Total Cost
Hot Dogs	20%	45	6.00	1.20	4.80	270.00	54
Hamburgers	20%	55	9.00	1.80	7.20	495.00	99
Corn dogs	20%	35	6.50	1.30	5.20	227.50	45.5
					Total	$993	$199

Analysis:

In the first column, this is where I put the general categories for menu items the Food Truck will sell. Categories include hotdogs, hamburgers, and corndogs. Of course, there are further differentiating factors between menu items like toppings. However, for the sake of estimates, I use an average price for all items.

The second important item in the chart above would be "% Sales." The percent of sales are used to determine the cost of goods sold. The cost of goods sold is how much the Food Truck owner spends to make the menu items. To illustrate, the cost of goods sold may be the amount of money the Food Truck spent on hamburger rolls and hamburger meat.

Labor:

Every business that has ever been started that will ever be started needs some type of labor involved. Even if the labor is only the company owner, make sure to include the labor section and the expected dollar amount to be paid monthly.

Sample:

Labor				
Employee	**Number**	**Rate**	**Monthly Hours**	**Total Pay**
Salary		n/a	n/a	2,500
Manager	1	20.00	172	3,440
Employees	2	18.00	172	6,192
			Total	$9,632

Analysis:

When I create my labor template, "salary" is the amount of money the owner wishes to be compensated for their time and energy. Some owners may argue that they will not take a salary in the first year. However, lenders and investors, almost to the person, will want to see the owner take some kind of salary when the Food Truck starts. Because of this, the salary is always the first line in all of my labor financial models.

Following this line item would be managers and employees. As you can see in the example above, the structure will allow you to enter the number of managers in the average pay rate as well as the number of employees and their average pay rate. Again, we are embracing and exploiting the concept of averages.

Monthly Fixed Costs:

The monthly fixed cost segment should include any and all costs that the firm will spend continuously, monthly. Popular fixed costs may include rent, utilities, insurance, and advertising.

Sample:

Monthly Fixed Costs	
Monthly Costs	**Monthly Total**
Rent	-
Utilities	750
Office Expenses	120
Insurance	175
Accounting/legal	125
Advertising	650
Other	235
Monthly Total	$2,055

Analysis:

Fixed costs are definitely a misnomer. Just because we call them "fixed costs" does not mean the costs will not change monthly. The fixed costs title is more focused on the actual items being paid as compared to the same dollar amount paid each month.

When constructing the fixed costs segment, there are a couple of different theories that may be applied to the construction of the segment. First, some Food Truck owners prefer to leave fixed costs as the same dollar amount throughout the year and then add a growth estimate for the next year.

Other owners prefer to utilize a percent of sales approach. In this approach, costs that change monthly, such as utilities, office expenses, and "other," would be based on a percent of sales technique. In this technique, each variable line item would be divided by sales. For subsequent months fixed costs, the line items would be calculated by multiplying the percent found in the first month for the line item by sales in the following months. This technique is known as common sizing.

Growth Rates:

Growth rates are the percentages used to increase a line item due to growth or inflation. Not surprisingly, different sections of the financial estimates will grow at different paces. From this, the need for a section related to growth rates is needed.

Sample:

Growth Rates	
Growth Rate Sales 2 & 3	3.50%

Growth Rate Sales 4 & 5	1.50%
Growth Rate Cost of Goods	1.50%
Growth Rate Salary	1.50%
Growth Rate Labor	3.00%
Growth Advertising	1.00%
Growth Office	1.00%
Growth Utility	1.00%
Growth Legal	1.00%
Growth Insurance	1.00%
Growth Other	1.00%

Analysis:

My preference for the growth rates is to show different growth rates for each category. Labor is bound to grow at a different pace than say business insurance. This structure allows for the needed adjustments.

Misc. Information:

The miscellaneous information section is pretty much used as a catchall for adjusting various line items in the financial statements. This segment may include the tax rate, cost of capital for the organization, franchise royalty payments, etc.

Sample:

Misc. Information	
Tax Rate	20%
Cost of Capital	10%

Analysis:

In this section, I usually only include the tax rate and cost of capital. For most instances, the cost of capital is not really needed. However, the tax rate is essential for determining estimated taxes that the Food Truck will pay on a monthly and annual basis.

Loan Payment Calculation:

When obtaining a loan, banks often prefer to calculate the loan information using their proprietary software. However, the business owner should still use the Excel function for calculating payments and include the information in their financial statements. An important concept to keep in mind for the income statement is to make sure they subtract interest paid instead of the full monthly payment for the loan. Not only is this standard procedure for accounting, but it also helps to show increased revenues.

Sample:

Loan Information	
Loan Amount	(130,000.00)
Interest Rate	7%
Term	15
Payment	$1,168.48

Analysis:

In this example above, a loan is expected to be taken out for $130,000. The interest rate is expected to be 7% with a term of 15 years. As a result, the Food Truck owner will be expected to pay $1,168.48 monthly. As noted above, for the profit and loss statement as well as the income statement, the monthly interest payment is the portion used. To find the interest portion, the amortization schedule is needed.

Profit and Loss for 12 Months:

The profit and loss statement shows the revenues, costs, taxes, and profits for your business. My preference is to break up the 12-month profit and loss statement into monthly segments and then total each month quarterly. By doing this, the company owner can see the monthly growth projections, as well as the costs aligned with the projected revenues.

Business Plan Writing Tip:

When creating your 12-month profit and loss statement, make sure to always use Excel or some other spreadsheet. This will allow you to do calculations easily and duplicate your work month over month.

When creating your profit and loss statement, make sure to always start with your revenues and then align the cost of goods and other fixed costs with your monthly sales. By following this process, the business owner can see how much money the organization can make and what costs are involved with the process.

Sample:

Pro Forma Income Statement Year 1 Quarter 1			
Income Statement	Month 1	Month 2	Month 3	Quarter 1
Revenues	29,874	30,770	31,694	92,338
COGS	5,975	6,154	6,339	18,468
Gross Profit	23,899	24,616	25,355	73,871
Expenses				
Salary	2,500	2,500	2,500	7,500
Labor	9,632	9,632	9,632	28,896
Advertising	650	650	650	1,950
Office Expen.	120	124	127	371
Rent	-	-	-	-
Utilities	750	773	796	2,318
Legal / Account	125	125	125	375
Insurance	175	175	175	525
Depreciation	1,091	1,091	1,091	3,273
Other	235	235	235	705
Total Expenses	15,278	15,304	15,331	45,913
EBIT	8,622	9,312	10,024	27,958
Interest Expense	758	756	754	2,268
EBT	7,863	8,557	9,271	25,690
Taxes	1,573	1,711	1,854	5,138

Net Income	6,291	6,845	7,416	20,552

Analysis:

In this example, first, start with the revenues that are projected for the month. To give first-month revenues, I always go back to my expected daily sales. Using daily sales, I will then multiply the daily sales by 30 and the cost of goods by 30. This will give me my first-month sales and the cost of goods.

Next, identify the fixed costs aligned with the monthly sales and deduct them from the gross profits, which is just revenue subtracted by the cost of goods sold. Once this is complete, just subtract any interest expenses and taxes. This leaves the Food Truck's net income.

To determine the second-month profit and loss, first, start by multiplying the revenues by an expected monthly growth rate. Next, for costs that increase monthly, based on sales, use the common size financial document. For example, in the example above, the office expense was .4% of sales. From this, we would multiply .4% by the new revenues for the next 12-months to determine the expected office supplies costs. This practice would be used for labor, office expenses, and utilities, as well. Keep in mind, for some costs, such as rent, advertising, insurance, and salary; these costs will remain the same, usually, for the first 12-months.

Income Statement:

The income statement is simply the total of your 12 months profit and loss statements. In other words, the income statement shows the total revenues and costs for the first 12-months. Once this is complete, most income statements will then project revenues, costs, and profits for the next four years, giving the business owner a five-year income statement projection to review.

Business Plan Writing Tip:

When creating your income statement, my preference is to first construct a table showing quarterly profit and losses, as shown below. Next, total the quarterly profits and losses into an annual column. With this complete, create a table using the annual revenues, costs and include columns for years two through five. The next step is to utilize our growth projections, as noted earlier, and multiply each line item by the associated growth projection. This will result in a five-year income statement, as shown below.

Sample:

Pro Forma Income Statement Annual Summary					
Income Statement	Quarter 1	Quarter 2	Quarter 3	Quarter 4	Annual
Revenues	92,338	100,901	110,257	120,481	423,976
COGS	18,468	20,180	22,051	24,096	84,795
Gross Profit	73,871	80,720	88,205	96,384	339,181
	-	-	-	-	-
Expenses					
Salary Labor	7,500	7,500	7,500	7,500	30,000

	28,896	28,896	28,896	28,896	115,584
Advertising	1,950	1,950	1,950	1,950	7,800
Office Expen.	371	401	439	479	1,690
Rent	-	-	-	-	-
Utilities	2,318	2,509	2,742	2,996	10,566
Legal / Account	375	375	375	375	1,500
Insurance	525	525	525	525	2,100
Depreciation	3,273	3,273	3,273	3,273	13,090
Other	705	705	705	705	2,820
Total Expenses	45,913	46,134	46,404	46,699	185,150
	-	-	-	-	-
EBIT	27,958	34,586	41,801	49,685	154,031
Interest Expense	2,268	2,246	2,224	2,201	8,939
EBT	25,690	32,340	39,577	47,484	145,092
Taxes	5,138	6,468	7,915	9,497	29,018
Net Income	20,552	25,872	31,662	37,987	116,074

Pro Forma Income Statement - Base					
Income Statement	**Year 1**	**Year 2**	**Year 3**	**Year 4**	**Year 5**
Revenues	423,976	505,745	523,446	531,297	539,267

COGS	84,795	101,149	102,666	104,206	105,769
Gross Profit	339,181	404,596	420,779	427,091	433,498
Expenses					
Salary	30,000	30,450	30,907	31,370	31,841
Labor	115,584	119,052	122,623	126,302	130,091
Advertising	7,800	7,878	7,957	8,036	8,117
Office Expenses	1,690	2,030	2,050	2,071	2,092
Rent	-	-	-	-	-
Utilities	10,566	12,688	12,814	12,943	13,072
Legal / Accounting	1,500	1,515	1,530	1,545	1,561
Insurance	2,100	2,121	2,142	2,164	2,185
Depreciation	13,090	22,069	15,379	11,155	10,577
Other	2,820	2,848	2,877	2,905	2,935
Total Expenses	185,150	200,650	198,279	198,491	202,470
EBIT	154,031	203,945	222,500	228,600	231,027
Interest Expense	8,939	8,572	8,178	7,755	7,302
Earnings before taxes	145,092	195,374	214,323	220,845	223,725
Taxes	29,018	39,075	42,865	44,169	44,745
Net Income	116,074	156,299	171,458	176,676	178,980

Analysis:

I started with the quarterly expected profit and loss projections that we calculated in the 12-month profit and loss section. Next, I added together the quarterly projections to come up with the first-year income statement projection. Once this was completed, I used the growth rates discussed in the growth rate section to project the next four years' profit and losses in the income statement.

Balance Sheet:

The balance sheet is, for the most part, not absolutely needed in the business plan. This is because the projections for the balance sheet will almost always be significantly off as compared to actual results. However, for the diehard entrepreneurs looking to cover all aspects of their financial expectations, presented below is a sample balance sheet.

Business Plan Writing Tip:

When discussing the balance sheet, make sure to explicitly state that the projections for the financial statement may change based on sales, operations, and other business needs. I like to put the statement before the balance sheet because of the significant fluctuation between projected returns and the actual results in the balance sheet.

When discussing the balance sheet, make sure to highlight the cash position and retained earnings. The cash position is important because this will show the reader that you, as the owner, expect to have enough liquid assets to operate the organization for the short and long term. As for the retained earnings, this section is where your net profit, minus dividends paid, ties into your balance sheet.

If your retained earnings grow at the same pace as your net profits, then this shows that your company reinvests most of the profits earned. However, if the segment grows at a significantly slower pace as compared to your net income, then investors and bankers may ascertain that a significant amount of your net profits are being paid out to the founder as dividends or other owners.

Sample:

Balance Sheet - Pro Forma					
Assets	Year 1	Year 2	Year 3	Year 4	Year 5
Cash	167,758	340,971	522,267	704,141	887,874
Accts Receiv.	-	-	-	-	-
Inventories	7,066	8,429	8,556	8,684	8,814
Total Curr. Assets	174,824	349,400	530,823	712,825	896,688
PP&E	119,200	119,200	119,200	119,200	119,200
Less Deprec.	13,090	35,159	50,538	61,693	72,270
Net PP&E	106,110	84,041	68,662	57,507	46,930
Total Assets	280,934	433,441	599,485	770,332	943,618

Balance Sheet - Pro Forma					
Liabilities	Year 1	Year 2	Year 3	Year 4	Year 5
Accounts					

Pay	7,066	8,429	8,556	8,684	8,814
Notes Payable	745	714	681	646	609
Accruals	12,132	12,458	12,794	13,139	13,494
Total Current Liab.	19,943	21,602	22,031	22,469	22,917
Loans	124,917	119,467	113,623	107,356	101,215
Total Liabilities	144,860	141,069	135,654	129,826	124,132
Common Stock	20,000	20,000	20,000	20,000	20,000
Retained Earnings	116,074	272,373	443,831	620,506	799,487
Total Com. Equity	136,074	292,373	463,831	640,506	819,487
Total Liab & Equity	280,934	433,441	599,485	770,332	943,618

Analysis:

In the example above, the Food Truck owner can see that the retained earnings section of the balance sheet grows significantly year-over-year. This shows that the owner intends to reinvest a significant portion of their net profits back into the Food Truck. By doing this, the Food Truck owner increases the likelihood of success in the business.

Further, the example above showed the cash position grown significantly over five years. This also helps the Food Truck owner show that they fully expect enough liquidity to support operations for the short and long term.

Financial Ratios:

Financial ratios utilize a firm's financial projections to show how efficient or profitable and organization will be based on the owner's best estimate. Common financial ratios include:

- Return on equity
- Return on assets
- Current ratio
- Profit margin

Return on Equity - Almost all investors are crazy about return on equity. This is because the return on equity indicates to investors how much the company profited concerning equity invested. As shown below, the calculation for return on equity is net income divided by total equity. Investors want to see this ratio as high as possible and climbing over time. This is because either an organization is increasing its net income by using the same amount of equity invested, or the firm is using less equity to generate the same amount of money.

Formula:

$$ROE = Net\ Income\ /\ Total\ Equity$$

Return on Assets - In keeping with the profitability thing, the return on assets allows investors to assess how profitable our target organization is as compared to the total assets utilized by the organization. With this ratio, investors prefer to see a relatively high return on assets. This indicates that the organization is generating net profits from assets as a whole.

Formula:

$$ROA = Net\ Income\ /\ Total\ Assets$$

Current Ratio - One of the most popular financial ratios is the current ratio. The current ratio measures the amount of cash inflow (money coming into the business) over the last 12-months with the amount of cash outflow (bills that needed to be paid by the firm). From this measurement, we can determine whether the organization had enough money coming in to cover funds going out.

Formula:

Current Ratio = Current Assets / Current Liabilities

In the above formula, we can see that if a business has more current assets than current liabilities, the answer will always be greater than one. However, if a company has more current liabilities as compared to current assets, then the answer is going to be less than one.

Profit Margin - My personal favorite financial ratio is the profit margin. The profit margin ratio compares a firm's net income, or profits, with their revenues. Again, the higher this ratio, the better for investors. A distressing trend to be cognizant of, as an investor, is when the profit margin increases when revenues fall. This happens because management has taken it upon themselves to significantly cut costs within the organization. Unfortunately, this type of action is not sustainable. Further, cost-cutting often leads to long-term revenue decline.

Formula:

Profit Margin = Net Income / Total Revenues

Business Plan Writing Tip:

When writing the financial ratio section of the business plan, don't just provide the ratios, make sure to explain what the ratios actually mean. By doing this, the entrepreneur adds credibility to the calculations. Also, this will help show the importance of the ratios selected.

Sample:

Financial Ratios					
Ratios	**Year 1**	**Year 2**	**Year 3**	**Year 4**	**Year 5**
Liquidity					
Quick Ratio	8.41	15.78	23.71	31.34	38.74
Current Ratio	8.77	16.17	24.09	31.72	39.13
Efficiency Ratios					
Inventory Turnover	60.00	60.00	61.18	61.18	61.18
Asset Turnover	1.51	1.17	0.87	0.69	0.57
Payables Turnover	60.00	60.00	61.18	61.18	61.18
Stability Ratios					
Debt to Equity	92.35%	41.11%	24.64%	16.86%	12.43%
Interest Coverage	17.23	23.79	27.21	29.48	31.64
Profitability					
Return on Assets	41.32%	36.06%	28.60%	22.94%	18.97%
Return on Equity	85.30%	53.46%	36.97%	27.58%	21.84%
Gross Margin Ratio	20.00%	20.00%	19.61%	19.61%	19.61%
Operating Income Ratio	39.42%	44.69%	45.44%	45.13%	44.80%
Profit Margin	27.38%	30.90%	32.76%	33.25%	33.19%

Analysis:

In the sample above, the business owner expected to provide investors with a return on equity in the first year of 85.3%. As the organization grows, the return on equity is expected to decrease. Usually, this situation happens when the business owner continually reinvests their net profits. In other words, the business owner intends to utilize equity for growth opportunities as compared to taking on debt.

For the return on assets, the business owner in the scenario anticipates a 41.32% return on assets for the first year. This is anticipated to decline to 18.97% in year five. The reduction in return on assets may be partly due to holding a significant amount of cash. From the perspective of an investor, this may be of a minor concern because the excessive cash holding may be preferable than taking on additional risk for a startup Food Truck.

As for the current ratio, this shows that the business intends to have a significant cash position in the first year and grow this position for the next several years. As a result, the business owner will have more than enough current assets to pay for their current liabilities.

As for the profit margin, this also is projected to increase. Specifically, the profit margin is anticipated to grow from 27.38% in year 1 to 33.19% in year 5. This indicates that the business owner expects revenues to increase at a faster pace than the cost of goods and fixed costs.

Step 8 – Funding Request

The funding request section should include four important components, which are potential funding sources, funding terms, use of funds, and fund repayment.

Sample:

Funding Request

To start operations, funding of $150,000 in debt or equity from a bank or investor is required. Debt funding is expected to have a term of 15 to 20 years with an interest rate between 6% to 9%. Principle and interest payments will be made monthly, using profits from the business. For investors, a negotiated percentage of ownership in the Food Truck will be offered. Also, after the second year of profitability, investors will be compensated through semi-annually dividend payments from business cash flows.

Received funds will be used as follows:

Startup Costs	
Category	**Estimate**
Equity Investment	20,000.00
Loan	130,000.00
Initial Build Out	75,000
Working Capital	28,300.00
Cooking Equipment	25,000.00
Inventory	7,500.00
Supplies	2,500.00
Training	3,000.00

Office Equipment	1,200.00
Misc.	5,000.00
Misc. Licenses	2,500.00
Total	**150,000.00**

Potential Funding Sources:

The potential funding source, or sources, are all of the channels that the business owner may use to obtain funding for their organization. Popular funding sources include lending institutions, such as banks, private investors, and grants. Most recently, crowdfunding has become a popular source of financing, as well.

Business Plan Writing Tip:

Make sure to discuss every source that may be considered for funding. Common sources include investors and lending institutions, such as banks or credit unions. However, other funding sources are available, as well. These may include grants or crowdfunding opportunities.

Sample:

To start operations, funding of $150,000 in debt or equity from a bank or investor is required.

Analysis:

As shown in the example above, for this Food Truck owner, lending sources are limited to investors and lending institutions. If the owner decided to explore grants or crowdfunding opportunities, then the business plan should be updated to reflect these aspirations.

Funding Terms:

Funding terms are the range of terms that the company owner will entertain. Funding terms may include a range of interest rates that would be acceptable to the owner for a loan. As for investors, terms with this party is a little bit more complicated. From this, just stating that an equity position is negotiable often will suffice.

Business Plan Writing Tip:

In the funding term section, make sure to tell the potential lender or investor your expectations or parameters for funding. These parameters should include a dollar amount for the loan or equity investment, length of time for loan, expected interest rate, or offer for a percentage of the organization to potential investors.

Sample:

Debt funding is expected to have a term of 15 to 20 years with an interest rate between 6% to 9%.

<u>*And*</u>

For investors, a negotiated percentage of ownership in the Food Truck will be offered.

Analysis:

The dollar amount expected, or need is $150,000. For this particular segment, a specific dollar amount is highly recommended. However, in certain situations, a range of funding may be acceptable. Just make sure to explain why the range of funds is needed.

The second part is related to the term expected for the loan, which is between 15 and 20 years. For most other instances of the business funding request, ranges are more than acceptable; they are actually recommended to be honest.

Use of Funds:

The use of funds section is where the business owner shows the investor or lender where their money will be spent. A common use of funds includes working capital, which is money needed for general operations, the buildout of a facility, if you need to rent an office space or retail space, and purchasing inventory.

Business Plan Writing Tip:

When I write a use of funds section, I always put the information in a spreadsheet and show a total at the bottom. Further, when categorizing the use of funds, try to use broad categories, such as office equipment, storage equipment, etc. By staying general with the categories, this allows the company owner to use the funds as needed, but within the general budget.

Sample:

Startup Costs	
Category	Estimate
Equity Investment	20,000.00
Loan	130,000.00
Initial Build Out	75,000
Working Capital	28,300.00
Cooking Equipment	25,000.00
Inventory	7,500.00
Supplies	2,500.00
Training	3,000.00
Office Equipment	1,200.00
Misc.	5,000.00
Misc. Licenses	2,500.00
Total	**150,000.00**

Analysis:

In the example provided, my use of funds section is broken into segments to help with budgeting purposes. The segment utilized were equipment, inventory, supplies, etc. Not only does this show a well-thought-out startup funding structure, but this also helps the investor or loan officer ascertain whether some of the budgetary segments are in line with expectations.

Fund Repayment:

The fund repayment section will tell the investor or loan officer/underwriter how the loan or equity investment will be rewarded. For the most part, dividends and loan payments will be paid from profits in the business. This may seem like common sense to you and me. However, surprisingly enough, some people actually pay funds from other businesses or even from retirement accounts. By explaining how the funds will be repaid, the investor or loan officer will have a full picture of how their investment will be compensated.

Business Plan Writing Tip:

When writing this section, I prefer to have the fund repayment information addressed in the final paragraph. This allows the investing parties to understand the totality of the funding situation before being introduced to the repayment segment.

Sample:

Principle and interest payments will be made monthly, using profits from the business. For investors, a negotiated percentage of ownership in the Food Truck will be offered. Also, after the second year of profitability, investors will be compensated through semi-annually dividend payments from business cash flows.

Analysis:

In the example provided, funds used to repay vested parties are clearly stated in the funding request. Further, principal and interest payments come from profits in the Food Truck monthly. As for investors, their compensation will also come from cash flow in the Food Truck, but only after the second-year of profitability.

Step 9 – Executive Summary

The executive summary is the first section that a business owner should present to the interested party. When I write my executive summaries, they are always an abbreviated version of the business plan. By doing this, essentially, a business owner has two documents. The first document may be considered an executive summary. This will briefly explain, in broad terms, what the company is about, the menu items offered, differentiated items provided, financial outlook, and funds needed to start operations or grow the organization.

Company and Product:

The company and product/service section should briefly summarize the organization and product and or service being offered.

Business Plan Writing Tip:

When I write this section, I will always copy and paste my company summary and product description under the heading for the executive summary. Next, I literally just start deleting lines to reduce the content to approximately a paragraph.

For the second paragraph, I will then summarize the rest of the company description section of the business plan, such as competitive advantage, hours of operation, number of employees, and any other critical pieces of information that I want to show upfront about the business concept.

Sample:

Food Truck Summary: ABC Food Truck will be a limited liability corporation located at 123 Broadway St. in Orlando, FL. The business owner(s) will be John Smith. Our American food-themed food truck will focus on popular American menu items such as hamburgers, hotdogs, and corndogs. As for a side menu items, we will provide hand-cut French fries, home-made chili, and baked beans. To comply with local regulations, our food truck will use an established commercial kitchen for food prep. The geographic area of service will be approximately a 50-mile radius from Orlando, Florida. The hours of operation will depend on the venue, typically, evening hours and weekends.

Analysis:

In the summary section, I like to succinctly describe the company using information from the company description section. Important information will include the company name, menu items sold, geographic location serviced, and business owner.

Target Market:

The target market, as noted earlier in the book, is a demographic or group of individuals that may frequently visit our business.

Business Plan Writing Tip:

For this section, I just simply note the target market and eliminate any additional information as to why the selection was made.

Sample:

Our primary target market will be young, blue color works. Specifically, families between the ages of 25 to 35. As for the secondary target market, this will be children between the ages of 7 and 12.

Analysis:

The sample shows the type of worker and age bracket of our target market and little else.

Financial Highlights:

The financial highlights section of the executive summary should stay focused on how the business will perform financially over the next 12-months. Because of this limited focus, popular inclusions in the financial highlight summary section would be related to first-year annual profits, expenses aligned with these prophets, and net profits expected.

Business Plan Writing Tip:

I like to keep this section to approximately four lines. Further, I always first introduce the revenues and then the cost aligned with the revenues. With this done, I finished the paragraph with net profits and the profit margin ratio. The succinct financial summary shows investors or loan officers the organization's potential profits in short order.

Sample:

The financial projections are based on market research and empirical examination of the local Food Truck industry. For the next year, we project revenues of approximately $423,976. The estimated expense costs will be $269,945. After taxes, we estimate a net profit of $116,074. This leads to a profit margin of approximately 27.38%.

Analysis:

The summarized version of the financial summary is definitely short and sweet. The most important aspects of the financial statements are included in the short paragraph. Further, the structure of the financial summary almost tells a story. First, it starts with revenues, then shows the cost involved with the revenues. Once the costs are deducted, then the profits are shown. Finally, a real quick ratio was presented, as well.

Funding:

Differing from the other sections in the executive summary, the funding section should be almost identical to the funding section in the business plan, except the cost breakdown. Not surprisingly, investors want to know how much money the company needs and how they will be repaid. There is no skimping on details here.

Business Plan Writing Tip:

The section should be written in terms similar to, or identical to, the funding section of the business plan, as noted above.

Sample:

To start operations, funding of $150,000 in debt or equity from a bank or investor is required. Debt funding is expected to have a term of 15 to 20 years with an interest rate between 6% to 9%. Principle and interest payments will be made monthly, using profits from the business. For investors, a negotiated percentage of ownership in the Food Truck will be offered. Also, after the second year of profitability, investors will be compensated through semi-annually dividend payments from business cash flows.

Analysis:

Not much need for analysis. Just copy and paste and ignore the startup cost. You are now ready to go.

Step 10 – Appendix

The appendix section is used for charts, graphs, and other documents that support the business plan.

Resumes:

For almost all business plans, I will include the business owner's resume in the appendix section. The resume helps to support experiences noted in the management and organization section of the business plan.

Business Plan Writing Tip:

When including a resume in a business plan, stay away from the pictures and fancy fonts. Usually, the reader is more interested in understanding the business owners' experiences and education related to the proposed business.

Sample:

Paul Borosky

XXX Rachelle Dr. Apt XXX - Sanford, FL. 32771 - (321) 948-**** – Paulb@Qualitybusinessplan.com

Professional Experience

Quality Business Plan — **Business Consulting –**
Business Plan Writing

Sanford, Fl. / Online
statements.
October 2010 - Present

* Prepared pro forma financial

* Research various
industries for trends, revenues, and growth projections.
* Calculate various financial
ratios such as Return on Equity and Current Ratio.
* Write business plans for
current and prospective businesses.

XXX High school   **Entrepreneurship / Microsoft Office / Computer Programming Instructor**

Durham, NC.

August, 2014 – October, 2016

* Prepare lesson plans for
Excel, Word, Visual Basic, and other classes.
* Assign and grade various
assignments.
* Provide in-depth student
feedback in residential settings.
* Assist students through
numerous stages of learning.

XXX College   **Resident and Online Adjunct Finance / Entrepreneurship Instructor**

Ocala, Fl.

June, 2013 – December 2016

* Prepare lesson plans for
residential class.
* Assign and grade various
finance assignments.
* Provide in-depth student
feedback in residential and online settings.
* Assist students through
numerous stages of learning.
* Subject Matter Expert –
Created and Designed college level finance classes.

Walt Disney World Resorts   **Quick Service Food -**
Supervisor

Orlando, Fl.

April, 2011-Jan, 2013

* Prepared guest meals in fast
pace environment.
* Display exceptional customer
service to guest.

* Daily practice Disney's leader basics.

* Lead other cast members by example and instruction.

Education

Northcentral University	DBA, Management – Doctoral Candidate Ongoing
Webster University	Finance – 21 Master level credit hours 2011
Webster University (MBA)	Masters in Business Administration 2010
Barry University	Bachelors in Professional Studies with specialization in Administration 2009
Seminole State College	AA Degree 2002

Training and Skills

Blackboard Learning System	Rasmussen College 2016
Microsoft PowerPoint Certified	Certiport 2016
Microsoft Excel Certified	Certiport 2016
Microsoft Word Certified	Certiport 2015
Canvas Learning System	Voyager High School 2015
NC Department of Education	Temporary Professional Educator's License 2014
Angel Learning System	Rasmussen College 2013
Fl. Department of Education	Statement of Status of Eligibility – Business (grades 6-12) 2013

Online Faculty Training   Rasmussen College
                                                  2013

Salesforce   Training for Salesforce software
                                                  2013

Summary

In summary, the business plan writing process is definitely long, tedious, and detailed, to say the least. However, by following the discussed business plan writing process in this book AND by using the sample and template provided, you now have the tools and training to complete your very own business plan!

Best of luck with your endeavor!

Food Truck Business Plan Sample

Executive Summary

Food Truck Summary: ABC Food Truck will be a limited liability corporation located at 123 Broadway St. in Orlando, FL. The business owner(s) will be John Smith. Our American food-themed food truck will focus on popular American menu items such as hamburgers, hotdogs, and corndogs. As for a side menu items, we will provide hand-cut French fries, home-made chili, and baked beans. To comply with local regulations, our food truck will use an established commercial kitchen for food prep. The geographic area of service will be approximately a 50-mile radius from Orlando, Florida. The hours of operation will depend on the venue, typically, evening hours and weekends.

Competitive Advantages: ABC Food Truck will have specific competitive advantages once our firm starts operations. Specifically, our Food Truck will use local, farm-fresh organic produce and dairy products when possible.

Target Market: Our primary target market will be young, blue color works. Specifically, families between the ages of 25 to 35. As for the secondary target market, this will be children between the ages of 7 and 12.

Financial Highlights: The financial projections are based on market research and empirical examination of the local Food Truck industry. For the next year, we project revenues of approximately $423,976. The estimated expense costs will be $269,945. After taxes, we estimate a net profit of $116,074. This leads to a profit margin of approximately 27.38%.

Funding Request: To start operations, funding of $150,000 in debt or equity from a bank or investor is required. Debt funding is expected to have a term of 15 to 20 years with an interest rate between 6% to 9%. Principle and interest payments will be made monthly, using profits from the business. For investors, a negotiated percentage of ownership in the Food Truck will be offered. Also, after the second year of profitability, investors will be compensated through semi-annually dividend payments from business cash flows.

Food Truck Description

Food Truck Summary

ABC Food Truck will be a limited liability corporation located at 123 Broadway St. in Orlando, FL. The business owner(s) will be John Smith. Our American food-themed food truck will focus on popular American menu items such as hamburgers, hotdogs, and corndogs. As for a side menu items, we will provide hand-cut French fries, home-made chili, and baked beans. The drink selection will include Coca-Cola products.

To comply with local regulations, our food truck will use an established commercial kitchen for food prep. The geographic area of service will be approximately a 50-mile radius from Orlando, Florida. The hours of operation will depend on the venue, typically, evening hours and weekends.

Competitive Advantages

ABC Food Truck will have specific competitive advantages once our firm starts operations. First, our Food Truck will use local, farm-fresh organic produce and dairy products when possible. No other competitor in the area has committed to this business model. By doing this, not only will our organization support local farmers, but we will also be helping to protect the environment by using organic raw material.

Products/Services Description

All of our hamburgers will be 100% Angus beef. Toppings may include lettuce, tomatoes, pickles, onions, a wide selection of cheeses, and different sauces like mayonnaise, spicy mustard, and Thousand Island dressing.

Hotdogs:

For our hot dog menu, we focus on creative toppings like homemade chili, sauerkraut, Cheez whiz, ketchup, mustard, and bread and butter pickles.

Side items:

The side item selection will include hand-cut French fries, homemade chili, coleslaw, baked beans, and cornbread.

Beverages:

Our drink supplier will be Coca-Cola. From this, product selections will include Coca-Cola, Diet Coke, Sprite, power aid, and Mr. Pibb.

For a full menu selection, please review Appendix A.

Pricing Strategy

Our pricing structure will be focused on the best value strategy. For this strategy, our management team will continually research prices of comparable food and drink menu items offered by local competitors in the area. From this research, we will create base menu item prices using the averages of competitors in the area. Next, our organization will make menu item price adjustments based on the quality of ingredients, the ambiance of the competitors' eateries, and overall menu selection as compared to ours. The end objective is to have all of our menu item prices competitively priced using the best value strategic model.

Business Models

Operations:

Our operational structure will seek to achieve a quick-service Food Truck's speed of service while offering high-quality meals that would rival a traditional fast-food dining experience. As a customer approaches our food truck, they will be met with our menu posted on the truck or chalkboard stand out front. This will allow visitors to decide upon their favorite dish before approaching the order window.

At the order window, our customers will be able to point to and select food items for purchase. Once the selection process is complete, we cook the items and bring the food to the "pickup" window for payment. In total, the process for each guest should be less than three minutes.

Hours of Operations:

Our hours of operations business model will be structured to ensure our Food Truck customers' needs are met at a convenient time. From this, our organization will be open based on venue operating hours. For example, if a food truck rally is held from 4 PM to 8 PM, then our operating hours will reflect this timeframe.

Location

As previously stated, our location will be in the Orlando, Florida, area. The proposed location size of the food truck will be about 200 square feet. Approximately three-quarters of the area will be dedicated to cooking and prep operations. The rest of the area will be devoted to storage, equipment, and driving area.

As for competition, this area has few other American-themed food trucks within a several miles radius. This will enable us to capture a significant portion of market share in the area.

Future Plans

Within the next 24 months, our firm will open new regions in the Central Florida and North Florida areas. The new food truck service areas and timeframe will be based on funding, leadership availability, and other factors. Further, our management team will introduce new menu items within the next 12 months. These menu items will be selected based on customer demand, how well the menu item will complement the current offering, and the availability of fresh ingredients.

Business Objectives and Time Line

1 - 3 Months

- Obtain investor funding.
- Identify the food truck and negotiate a purchase agreement.
- Engage in buildout activities.
- Hire employees.
- Start the advertising campaign.
- Open for business.

3 - 6 Months

- Document critical business models in the standard operating procedures manual.
- Survey customers about the menu and service.
- Evaluate marketing strategy.
- Evaluate business models.

6 - 12 Months

- Implement optimized marketing strategies.
- Implement optimized business models.
- Evaluate survey results and prepare a plan of action based on results.
- Examine external environment for market opportunities.

Mission Statement

"Our Food Truck's mission is to provide trending American-style foods; hot, fresh, and fast."

Vision Statement

"Deliver world-class trending American-style foods delights on a national arena."

Value Statement
- Honesty.
- Fair prices.
- High-quality dishes.
- Technical innovations

Keys to Success
- Innovative marketing.
- Skilled workers.
- Optimize operations.
- Service customers changing wants.

Target Market

Primary Target Market

Our primary target market will be young, blue color works. Specifically, families between the ages of 25 to 35. This demographic was selected because of their propensity to enjoy American-style foods at community events and other gatherings.

Secondary Target Market

As for the secondary target market, this will be children between the ages of 7 and 12. This demographic was selected because they tend to accompany parents to community events and other festivals.

Target Market Growth

Based on research from the website ABC, the current blue color work force in ABC City is 250,000 people. The U.S. Census Bureau has noted that the city's population increased by 1.3% annually over the last five years. Based on this factor, our Food Truck owner expects a similar growth rate for the next five years. From this, the target market formulation will be 253,250 within the next 12 months. In two years, our target market population will expand to 256,543 people.

Market Analysis

Industry Overview

Food trucks would fall under the umbrella of the street vendors industry. The street vendor industry sells quick-service type options like ethnic foods, ice creams, coffees, and even memorabilia from a mobile-type location. Revenues for the street vendors industry, as a whole, should exceed $3.5 billion next year. In the last five years, industry experts have found that the annual growth rate was approximately 4%. However, in the next five years, the street vendor industry growth rate should slow to about 1.5%.

Industry Statistics

- The street vendor industry is one of the few food service industries that are growing at an above-average growth rate.
- Food truck operators can change their menus to better meet the changing tastes of consumers as compared to traditional brick-and-mortar restaurants.
- Because of the popularity and growth of the industry, new rules and regulations from local and state legislators should be expected.

Threats, Trends, and Opportunities

An important threat to the industry would be related to the overall economy. Currently, job growth and employment are at all-time-highs. From this, people have enough discretionary funds to afford to dine out. Unfortunately, in the event of an economic recession, as discretionary funds for people decrease, profits for the Food Truck industry may show a correlated effect.

As for an opportunity, casual dinners are increasingly selecting "mom and pop" Food Trucks over chain restaurants due to better service, limited time for purchasing menu items, and appealing menu selections. This allows for startup Food Trucks to enter the market place and gain a loyal following.

Finally, trends in the Food Truck industry may be found in technological innovations. Technological innovations may help Food Truck owners offer better-quality foods or enhanced service for premium prices.

Keys to Success

To be successful in the Food Truck industry, competitors need to focus on hiring skilled employees. In other words, small businesses must employ and retain qualified and well-trained workers. Qualifications may not necessarily be in traditional schooling. However, experience with kitchen prep, serving, and driving are necessitated to ensure that a guest has a memorable visit to a Food Truck.

SWOT Analysis

Strengths	Weakness
•Management experience.	•Startup Food Truck.
•Documented plans.	•Untested business location.
•Themed Food Truck concept.	
• Training program.	

Opportunities	Threats
•Community involvement	•Local competitors
•Appeal to a wide variety of clientele.	•Susceptible to economic downturn.
•Location	
•Brand building	

Competitive Analysis

XYZ Food Truck is a "mom and pop" Food Truck in the Orlando, Florida area. The Food Truck was founded in 1984 and prides itself on its changing menu selection. As for services, the food truck offers a limited menu, focused on lunch and dinner. Based on a Google search, customers have had mixed reviews. Most reviews seemed satisfied with the food quality and service. However, some past customers complained that the cleanliness of the kitchen was lacking.

Organization and Management

Management Summary

John Smith, Sr., MBA., is the founder and CEO of ABC Food Truck. He has started and managed numerous successful small Food Trucks over the last ten years. Food Trucks started, and managed, includes a breakfast cafe, food truck, and 24-hour diner. For each business, he was responsible for all aspects of the organization, from marketing to strategic planning.

Job Responsibilities

CEO:
- Create and execute marketing strategies for business growth.
- Align business strategies with the vision statement.
- Negotiating contracts with vendors.
- Ensure legal compliance for the business.
- Continually examine the firm's external environment for new market opportunities.

General Manager:
- Control inventory to ensure optimal levels are attained.
- Manage day-to-day operations of the Food Truck.
- Interview and hire new employees.
- Assist in the onboarding process for new employees.

Window Attendant:
- Smile and greet customers as they approached the truck window.
- Explain menu items and ingredients.
- Collect payment for food.
- Prepare and deliver orders to the customer.

- Work with the kitchen team to ensure high-quality food products.

Food preparer:
- Prepare all menu items based on the ingredient list.
- Follow all handwashing and other sanitary policies and procedures.
- Prepare food item prep.
- Make all menu requests accurately and adjust to customer's preferences.

Organizational Chart

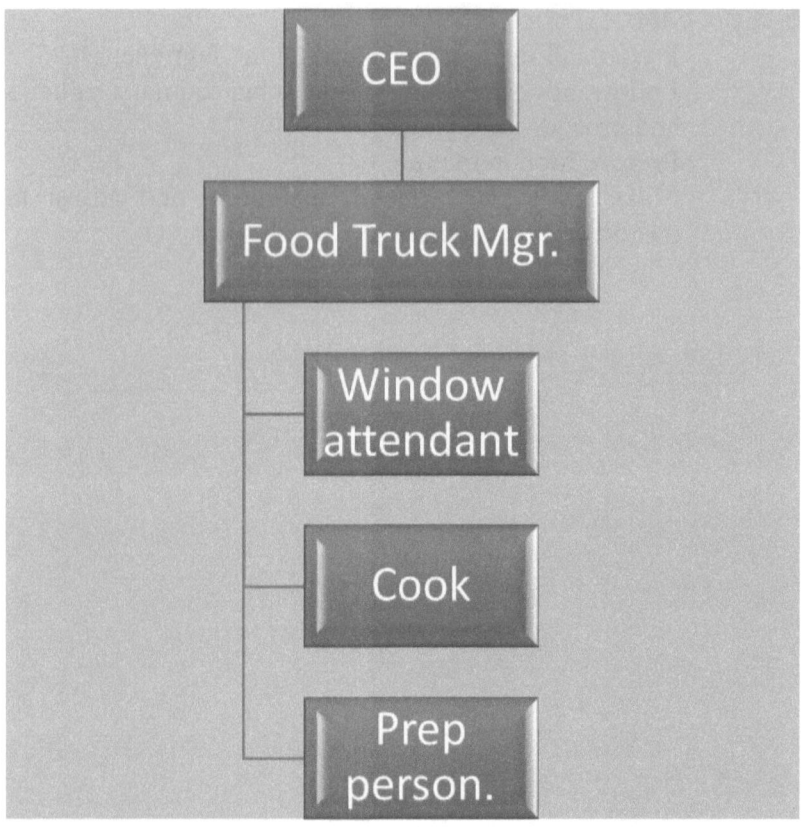

Marketing

Marketing Objectives and Keys to Success

Objectives

Market penetration.

Brand awareness.

Meet customers' changing needs.

Create marketing synergy

Keys to Success

Selecting appropriate marketing channels.

Continually keep customers engaged with our marketing material.

Periodically evaluate marketing actions for optimization.

Traditional Marketing

Our first traditional marketing channel will include a professionally designed vehicle wrap for the Food Truck. This vehicle wrap will include our Food Truck name, logo, and slogan. Further, prominent colors will include black, gold, and white. The objective of the signage is to let potential customers know our Food Truck's theme and possible menu items offered.

Internet Marketing

The importance of a professionally designed website cannot be understated. To exploit this opportunity, the ABC Food Truck will create and maintain a website and Yelp listing. The objective of the strategy is to effectively communicate our Food Truck's theme and highlight our menu items.

Social Media Marketing

ABC Food Truck's social media advertising will include Instagram, Twitter, and Facebook. Using a three-channel approach to social media will ensure our message reaches a broad audience, which will include our target market. Also, several potential customers will receive an advertising message on multiple social media outlets. This should exceed the needed repetition of our message to a broad audience as well as our target market. The marketing message will focus on our Food Truck menu items offered and possible weekly specials.

Financial Projections

Financial Assumptions

Our financial projections have several assumptions based on research and management's expectation of potential sales and costs.

- All financial projections are based on management and or owner(s) professional expectations of sales and expenses for the foreseeable future.

- In the first 12 months, sales should increase by approximately 5% each month. In months 13 to 24, sales growth should slow to approximately .3% per month. For years three through five, sales are expected to grow by 4.5%.

- The cost of goods or variable costs are expected to be approximately 30.21% of total sales.

- The initial advertising budget will be $650. Advertising is projected to increase by approximately 1% per year. This is to ensure maximum utilization of the firm's property and equipment.

- Cost projections were calculated using a common size model. This practice is typical for financial modeling.

- The tax rate was assumed to be 20%. Fluctuation in the tax rate will have a direct impact on net profits.

- The initial funding needed is $150,000. An increase/decrease in amount will impact the net present value and internal rate of return.

- The starting cash balance needed is $28,300 for working capital.

- A cash account was used to balance assets with liabilities and equity.

Financial Summary

The financial projections are based on market research and empirical examination of the local Food Truck industry. For the next year, we project revenues of approximately $423,976. The estimated expense costs will be $269,945. After taxes, we estimate a net profit of $116,074. This leads to a profit margin of approximately 27.38%. As our brand continues to grow, second-year progression is anticipated to yield a net income of approximately $156,299. Within five years, net income should exceed $178,980.

Startup Costs

Startup Costs	
Category	Estimate
Equity Investment	20,000.00
Loan	130,000.00
Initial Build Out	75,000
Working Capital	28,300.00
Cooking Equipment	25,000.00
Inventory	7,500.00
Supplies	2,500.00
Training	3,000.00
Office Equipment	1,200.00
Misc.	5,000.00
Misc. Licenses	2,500.00
Total	150,000.00

Daily Revenues

Revenue Generators							
Daily Sales	% Sales	Num.	Price	Cost	Profit	Total Rev.	Total Cost
Hot Dogs	20%	45	6.00	1.20	4.80	270.00	54
Hamburgers	20%	55	9.00	1.80	7.20	495.00	99
Corn dogs	20%	35	6.50	1.30	5.20	227.50	45.5
					Total	$993	$199

Labor

Labor				
Employee	Number	Rate	Monthly Hours	Total Pay
Salary		n/a	n/a	2,500
Manager	1	20.00	172	3,440
Employees	2	18.00	172	6,192
			Total	$9,632

Monthly Fixed Costs

Monthly Fixed Costs	
Monthly Costs	Monthly Total
Rent	-
Utilities	750
Office Expenses	120
Insurance	175

Accounting/legal	125
Advertising	650
Other	235
Monthly Total	$2,055

Growth Rates

Growth Rates	
Growth Rate Sales 2 & 3	3.50%
Growth Rate Sales 4 & 5	1.50%
Growth Rate Cost of Goods	1.50%
Growth Rate Salary	1.50%
Growth Rate Labor	3.00%
Growth Advertising	1.00%
Growth Office	1.00%
Growth Utility	1.00%
Growth Legal	1.00%
Growth Insurance	1.00%
Growth Other	1.00%

Misc. Information

Misc. Information	
Tax Rate	20%
Cost of Capital	10%

Loan Payment Calculations

Loan Information	
Loan Amount	(130,000.00)
Interest Rate	7%
Term	15
Payment	$1,168.48

Profit and Loss Quarter 1

Pro Forma Income Statement Year 1 Quarter 1			
Income Statement	Month 1	Month 2	Month 3	Quarter 1
Revenues	29,874	30,770	31,694	92,338
COGS	5,975	6,154	6,339	18,468
Gross Profit	23,899	24,616	25,355	73,871
Expenses				
Salary	2,500	2,500	2,500	7,500
Labor	9,632	9,632	9,632	28,896
Advertising	650	650	650	1,950
Office Expen.	120	124	127	371
Rent	-	-	-	-
Utilities	750	773	796	2,318
Legal / Account	125	125	125	375
Insurance	175	175	175	525
Depreciation	1,091	1,091	1,091	3,273
Other	235	235	235	705
Total Expenses	15,278	15,304	15,331	45,913
EBIT	8,622	9,312	10,024	27,958
Interest Expense	758	756	754	2,268

EBT	7,863	8,557	9,271	25,690
Taxes	1,573	1,711	1,854	5,138
Net Income	6,291	6,845	7,416	20,552

Profit and Loss Quarter 2

Pro Forma Income Statement Year 1 Quarter 2				
Income Statement	Month 4	Month 5	Month 6	Quarter 2
Revenues	32,644	33,624	34,632	100,901
COGS	6,529	6,725	6,926	20,180
Gross Profit	26,116	26,899	27,706	80,720
Expenses				
Salary	2,500	2,500	2,500	7,500
Labor	9,632	9,632	9,632	28,896
Advertising	650	650	650	1,950
Office Expen.	127	135	139	401
Rent	-	-	-	-
Utilities	796	844	869	2,509
Legal / Account	125	125	125	375
Insurance	175	175	175	525
Depreciation	1,091	1,091	1,091	3,273
Other	235	235	235	705
Total Expenses	15,331	15,387	15,416	46,134

EBIT	10,785	11,512	12,290	34,586
Interest Expense	751	749	746	2,246
EBT	10,034	10,763	11,543	32,340
Taxes	2,007	2,153	2,309	6,468
Net Income	8,027	8,611	9,235	25,872

Profit and Loss Quarter 3

Pro Forma Income Statement Year 1 Quarter 3				
Income Statement	Month 7	Month 8	Month 9	Quarter 3
Revenues	35,671	36,742	37,844	110,257
COGS	7,134	7,348	7,569	22,051
Gross Profit	28,537	29,393	30,275	88,205
Expenses				
Salary	2,500	2,500	2,500	7,500
Labor	9,632	9,632	9,632	28,896
Advertising	650	650	650	1,950
Office Expen.	139	148	152	439
Rent	-	-	-	-
Utilities	869	922	950	2,742
Legal / Account	125	125	125	375
Insurance	175	175	175	525
Depreciation				

	1,091	1,091	1,091	3,273
Other	235	235	235	705
Total Expenses	15,416	15,478	15,510	46,404
EBIT	13,121	13,915	14,765	41,801
Interest Expense	744	741	739	2,224
EBT	12,377	13,174	14,026	39,577
Taxes	2,475	2,635	2,805	7,915
Net Income	9,902	10,539	11,221	31,662

Profit and Loss Quarter 4

Pro Forma Income Statement Year 1 Quarter 4				
Income Statement	**Month 10**	**Month 11**	**Month 12**	**Quarter 4**
Revenues	38,979	40,148	41,353	120,481
COGS	7,796	8,030	8,271	24,096
Gross Profit	31,183	32,119	33,082	96,384
Expenses				
Salary	2,500	2,500	2,500	7,500
Labor	9,632	9,632	9,632	28,896
Advertising	650	650	650	1,950
Office Expen.	152	161	166	479
Rent	-	-	-	-
Utilities	950	1,008	1,038	2,996

Legal / Account	125	125	125	375
Insurance	175	175	175	525
Depreciation	1,091	1,091	1,091	3,273
Other	235	235	235	705
Total Expenses	15,510	15,577	15,612	46,699
EBIT	15,673	16,542	17,470	49,685
Interest Expense	736	734	731	2,201
EBT	14,937	15,808	16,739	47,484
Taxes	2,987	3,162	3,348	9,497
Net Income	11,950	12,646	13,391	37,987

Income Statement

Pro Forma Income Statement - Base					
Income Statement	Year 1	Year 2	Year 3	Year 4	Year 5
Revenues	423,976	505,745	523,446	531,297	539,267
COGS	84,795	101,149	102,666	104,206	105,769
Gross Profit	339,181	404,596	420,779	427,091	433,498
Expenses					
Salary	30,000	30,450	30,907	31,370	31,841
Labor	115,584	119,052	122,623	126,302	130,091
Advertising	7,800	7,878	7,957	8,036	8,117

	Year 1	Year 2	Year 3	Year 4	Year 5
Office Expenses	1,690	2,030	2,050	2,071	2,092
Rent	-	-	-	-	-
Utilities	10,566	12,688	12,814	12,943	13,072
Legal / Accounting	1,500	1,515	1,530	1,545	1,561
Insurance	2,100	2,121	2,142	2,164	2,185
Depreciation	13,090	22,069	15,379	11,155	10,577
Other	2,820	2,848	2,877	2,905	2,935
Total Expenses	185,150	200,650	198,279	198,491	202,470
EBIT	154,031	203,945	222,500	228,600	231,027
Interest Expense	8,939	8,572	8,178	7,755	7,302
Earnings before taxes	145,092	195,374	214,323	220,845	223,725
Taxes	29,018	39,075	42,865	44,169	44,745
Net Income	116,074	156,299	171,458	176,676	178,980

Balance Sheet

Balance Sheet - Pro Forma					
Assets	Year 1	Year 2	Year 3	Year 4	Year 5
Cash	167,758	340,971	522,267	704,141	887,874
Accts Receiv.	-	-	-	-	-
Inventories	7,066	8,429	8,556	8,684	8,814
Total Curr. Assets	174,824	349,400	530,823	712,825	896,688
PP&E					

	119,200	119,200	119,200	119,200	119,200
Less Deprec.	13,090	35,159	50,538	61,693	72,270
Net PP&E	106,110	84,041	68,662	57,507	46,930
Total Assets	280,934	433,441	599,485	770,332	943,618

Balance Sheet - Pro Forma					
Liabilities	Year 1	Year 2	Year 3	Year 4	Year 5
Accounts Pay	7,066	8,429	8,556	8,684	8,814
Notes Payable	745	714	681	646	609
Accruals	12,132	12,458	12,794	13,139	13,494
Total Current Liab.	19,943	21,602	22,031	22,469	22,917
Loans	124,917	119,467	113,623	107,356	101,215
Total Liabilities	144,860	141,069	135,654	129,826	124,132
Common Stock	20,000	20,000	20,000	20,000	20,000
Retained Earnings	116,074	272,373	443,831	620,506	799,487
Total Com. Equity	136,074	292,373	463,831	640,506	819,487
Total Liab & Equity	280,934	433,441	599,485	770,332	943,618

Financial Ratios

Financial Ratios					
Ratios	Year 1	Year 2	Year 3	Year 4	Year 5
Liquidity					
Quick Ratio	8.41	15.78	23.71	31.34	38.74
Current Ratio	8.77	16.17	24.09	31.72	39.13
Efficiency Ratios					
Inventory Turnover	60.00	60.00	61.18	61.18	61.18
Asset Turnover	1.51	1.17	0.87	0.69	0.57

Payables Turnover	60.00	60.00	61.18	61.18	61.18
Stability Ratios					
Debt to Equity	92.35%	41.11%	24.64%	16.86%	12.43%
Interest Coverage	17.23	23.79	27.21	29.48	31.64
Profitability					
Return on Assets	41.32%	36.06%	28.60%	22.94%	18.97%
Return on Equity	85.30%	53.46%	36.97%	27.58%	21.84%
Gross Margin Ratio	20.00%	20.00%	19.61%	19.61%	19.61%
Operating Income Ratio	39.42%	44.69%	45.44%	45.13%	44.80%
Profit Margin	27.38%	30.90%	32.76%	33.25%	33.19%

Funding Request

To start operations, funding of $150,000 in debt or equity from a bank or investor is required. Debt funding is expected to have a term of 15 to 20 years with an interest rate between 6% to 9%. Principle and interest payments will be made monthly, using profits from the business. For investors, a negotiated percentage of ownership in the Food Truck will be offered. Also, after the second year of profitability, investors will be compensated through semi-annually dividend payments from business cash flows.

Received funds will be used as follows:

Startup Costs	
Category	Estimate
Equity Investment	20,000.00
Loan	130,000.00
Initial Build Out	75,000
Working Capital	28,300.00
Cooking Equipment	25,000.00
Inventory	7,500.00
Supplies	2,500.00
Training	3,000.00
Office Equipment	1,200.00
Misc.	5,000.00
Misc. Licenses	2,500.00
Total	150,000.00

Appendix A: Resume

Paul Borosky

XXX Rachelle Dr. - Sanford, FL. 32771 - (321) 948-**** –
Paulb@Qualitybusinessplan.com

Professional Experience

Quality Business Plan   **Business Consulting –**
Business Plan Writing

Sanford, Fl. / Online   * Prepared pro forma financial statements.

October 2010 - Present   * Research various industries for trends, revenues, and growth projections.

* Calculate various financial ratios such as Return on Equity and Current Ratio.

* Write business plans for current and prospective businesses.

XXX High school   **Entrepreneurship / Microsoft Office / Computer Programming Instructor**

Durham, NC.   * Prepare lesson plans for Excel, Word, Visual Basic, and other classes.

August, 2014 – October, 2016   * Assign and grade various assignments.

* Provide in-depth student feedback in residential settings.

* Assist students through numerous stages of learning.

XXX College   **Resident and Online Adjunct Finance / Entrepreneurship Instructor**

Ocala, Fl.   * Prepare lesson plans for residential class.

June, 2013 – December 2016   * Assign and grade various finance assignments.

* Provide in-depth student feedback in residential and online settings.
* Assist students through numerous stages of learning.
* Subject Matter Expert – Created and Designed college level finance classes.

Walt Disney World Resorts Supervisor
Orlando, Fl.
April, 2011-Jan, 2013

Quick Service Food -

* Prepared guest meals in fast pace environment.
* Display exceptional customer service to guest.
* Daily practice Disney's leader basics.
* Lead other cast members by example and instruction.

Education

Northcentral University	DBA, Management – Doctoral Candidate	Ongoing
Webster University	Finance – 21 Master level credit hours	2011
Webster University (MBA)	Masters in Business Administration	2010
Barry University	Bachelors in Professional Studies with specialization in Administration	2009
Seminole State College	AA Degree	2002

Training and Skills

Blackboard Learning System	Rasmussen College	2016
Microsoft PowerPoint Certified	Certiport	2016

Microsoft Excel Certified	Certiport	2016
Microsoft Word Certified	Certiport	2015
Canvas Learning System	Voyager High School	2015
NC Department of Education	Temporary Professional Educator's License	2014
Angel Learning System	Rasmussen College	2013
Fl. Department of Education	Statement of Status of Eligibility – Business (grades 6-12)	2013
Online Faculty Training	Rasmussen College	2013
Salesforce	Training for Salesforce software	

Food Truck Business Plan Template (Includes Market Research!)

Executive Summary

Food Truck Summary: (Food Truck Name) is a (Business legal structure: limited liability corporation, sole proprietor, corporation) located in City, State. Our firm offers (products and services offered).

Our (type of Food Truck: American-themed, café, quick service) business specializes in (what will your Food Truck do best?).

(Name of the Food Truck) utilizes a (pricing strategy: best value, low price, premium) pricing model to ensure a fair price is offered to our customers. Our hours of operation are from (8:00 AM to 10 PM), (seven days a week, Monday – Friday, etc.). Our staff size is (four), including the owner. An important key to success in sustaining our Food Truck is to (important action that your Food Truck needs to take to succeed).

Target Market: Our primary target market will be (expected target market) between the ages of (age) to (age).

Financial Highlights: The financial projections are based on market research and empirical examination of the local Food Truck industry. For the next year, we project revenues of approximately $(a dollar amount). The estimated expense costs will be $(a dollar amount). After taxes, we estimate a net profit of $(a dollar amount). This leads to a profit margin of approximately (percent)%.

Funding Request: To start operations, funding of $(a dollar amount) in debt or equity from a bank or investor is required. Debt funding is expected to have a term of (15) to (20) years with an interest rate between (rate)% to (rate)%. Principle and interest payments will be made monthly, using profits from the business. For investors, a negotiated percentage of ownership in the Food Truck will be offered. Also, investors will be compensated through (when will dividends be paid: quarterly, semi-annually, etc.) dividend payments from business cash flows.

Food Truck Description

Food Truck Summary

(Food Truck Name) will be a (business legal structure: corporate, sole proprietor, limited liability corporation, corporate, etc.) located at (address) in (city, state). The business owner will be (your name). Our (type of Food Truck: café, casual dining, etc.) will offer on (menu items offered). Our hours of operation will be from (hours of operations).

Competitive Advantages

(Name of Food Truck) will have specific competitive advantages once our firm starts operations. First, (your main competitive advantage).

A second competitive advantage would be (second competitive advantage).

Menu Description

(Menu item 1)
Our *(Menu item 1)* will (describe menu item? What ingredients will be used?).

(Menu item 2)
Our *(Menu item 2)* will (describe menu item? What ingredients will be used?).

(Menu item 3)
Our *(Menu item 3)* will (describe menu item? What ingredients will be used?).

Pricing Strategy

Our pricing structure will be focused on a (low cost, best value, premium) pricing. The strategy was selected because (explain why you selected this pricing strategy).

Business Models

Operations:

Our operational structure will (describe how your Food Truck will operate).

Hours of Operations:

Our hours of operations business model will be structured to ensure our customers' needs are met at a convenient time. From this, our organization will be open from (hours of operation).

Location

As previously stated, our location will be at (Food Truck address). The proposed location size will be about (number) square feet. Approximately (percent) of the area will be dedicated to (what will be the main use of your facility). The rest of the area will be dedicated to (what else will your location be used for?).

As for competition, this area has about (number) competitors, offering similar menu items within a (number) square mile range.

Future Plans

Within the next (number) months, our firm will (discuss your future plans).

Business Objectives and Time Line

1 - 3 Months

- Objective 1
- Objective 2
- Objective 3
- Objective 4

3 – 6 Months

- Objective 1
- Objective 2
- Objective 3

6 – 12 Months

- Objective 1
- Objective 2
- Objective 3

Mission Statement

(Enter your mission statement here)

Vision Statement

(Enter your vision statement here)

Value Statement

- Value 1
- Value 2
- Value 3
- Value 4

Keys to Success

- Success 1
- Success 2
- Success 3
- Success 4

Target Market

Primary Target Market

Our primary target market will be (describe target market), specifically (male or female) between the ages of (age) to (age). This demographic was selected because (talk about why you selected this target market).

Secondary Target Market

As for the secondary target market, this will be (describe target market), specifically (male or female) between the ages of (age) to (age). This demographic was selected because (talk about why you selected this target market).

Target Market Growth

Based on research from (where did you get the target market growth information), the current target market population in the area is about (number) (individuals or businesses).

The (name of the source for researched information) has noted that the city's population has increased by (percent)% annually over the last (number) years. Based on this factor, our Food Truck expects a similar growth rate for the next (number) years. From this, the target market formulation will be (number) within the next (number) months. In two years, our target market population will expand to (number) (people or businesses).

Food Truck Market Analysis

In this market analysis, the industry, economy, and overall risk for the company will be analyzed for a better understanding of our external environment.

Industry: Food Truck Industry.

Food trucks would fall under the umbrella of the street vendors industry. The street vendor industry sells quick-service type options like ethnic foods, ice creams, coffees, and even memorabilia from a mobile-type location. Revenues for the street vendors industry, as a whole, should exceed $3.5 billion next year. In the last five years, industry experts have found that the annual growth rate was approximately 4%. However, in the next five years, the street vendor industry growth rate should slow to about 1.5%.

Industry Statistics

- The street vendor industry is one of the few food service industries that are growing at an above-average growth rate.
- Food truck operators can change their menus to better meet the changing tastes of consumers as compared to traditional brick-and-mortar restaurants.
- Because of the popularity and growth of the industry, new rules and regulations from local and state legislators should be expected.

Threats, Trends, and Opportunities

An important threat to the industry would be related to the overall economy. Currently, job growth and employment are at all-time-highs. From this, people have enough discretionary funds to afford to dine out. Unfortunately, in the event of an economic recession, as discretionary funds for people decrease, profits for the Food Truck industry may show a correlated effect.

As for an opportunity, casual dinners are increasingly selecting "mom and pop" Food Trucks over chain restaurants due to better service, limited time for purchasing menu items, and appealing menu selections. This allows for startup Food Trucks to enter the market place and gain a loyal following.

Finally, trends in the Food Truck industry may be found in technological innovations. Technological innovations may help Food Truck owners offer better-quality foods or enhanced service for premium prices.

Keys to Success

To be successful in the Food Truck industry, competitors need to focus on hiring skilled employees. In other words, small businesses must employ and retain qualified and well-trained workers. Qualifications may not necessarily be in traditional schooling. However, experience with kitchen prep, serving, and driving are necessitated to ensure that a guest has a memorable visit to a Food Truck.

Detailed SWOT Analysis

SWOT analysis:

Strengths
- Management experience.
- Strategic plans
- Trendy Food Truck concept

Weakness
- Startup company.
- Untested business location.

Opportunities
- Community involvement
- Appeal to a wide variety of clientele.
- Brand building

Threats
- Local competitors
- Susceptible to economic downturn.

Competitive Analysis

(Competitor 1)

(Competitor 1) is located (address). This is about (number) miles from our proposed location. The Food Truck offers (menu items). Based on a (Google or Facebook) search, important information was obtained. Previous customers, based on reviews, had mostly (good or bad) reviews. Specifically, the main area discussed was (what was most talked about on Google or Facebook reviews). As a result of the (Google or Facebook) reviews, the Food Truck currently has a (number) star rating.

(Competitor 2)

(Competitor 1) is located (address). This is about (number) miles from our proposed location. The Food Truck offers (menu items). Based on a (Google or Facebook) search, important information was obtained. Previous customers, based on reviews, had mostly (good or bad) reviews. Specifically, the main area discussed was (what was most talked about on Google or Facebook reviews). As a result of the (Google or Facebook) reviews, the Food Truck currently has a (number) star rating.

(Competitor 3)

(Competitor 1) is located (address). This is about (number) miles from our proposed location. The Food Truck offers (menu items). Based on a (Google or Facebook) search, important information was obtained. Previous customers, based on reviews, had mostly (good or bad) reviews. Specifically, the central area discussed was (what was most talked about on Google or Facebook reviews). As a result of the (Google or Facebook) reviews, the Food Truck currently has a (number) star rating.

Organization and Management

Management Summary

(Owner name) is the founder and CEO of (Food Truck name), which is a (business legal structure: sole proprietor, limited liability Food Truck, partnership, corporation). (He or she) has (number) years' experience in the Food Truck industry. From this experience, (owner name) has developed specialized critical skills needed to lead and manage this endeavor.

Job Responsibilities

CEO:
- Create and execute marketing strategies for business growth.
- Align business strategies with the vision statement.
- Negotiating contracts with vendors.
- Ensure legal compliance for the business.
- Continually examine the firm's external environment for new market opportunities.

General Manager:
- Control inventory to ensure optimal levels are attained.
- Manage day-to-day operations of the Food Truck.
- Interview and hire new employees.
- Assist in the onboarding process for new employees.

Window Attendant:
- Smile and greet customers as they approached the truck window.
- Explain menu items and ingredients.
- Collect payment for food.
- Prepare and deliver orders to the customer.

- Work with the kitchen team to ensure high-quality food products.

Food preparer:
- Prepare all menu items based on the ingredient list.
- Follow all handwashing and other sanitary policies and procedures.
- Prepare food item prep.
- Make all menu requests accurately and adjust to customer's preferences.

Organizational Chart

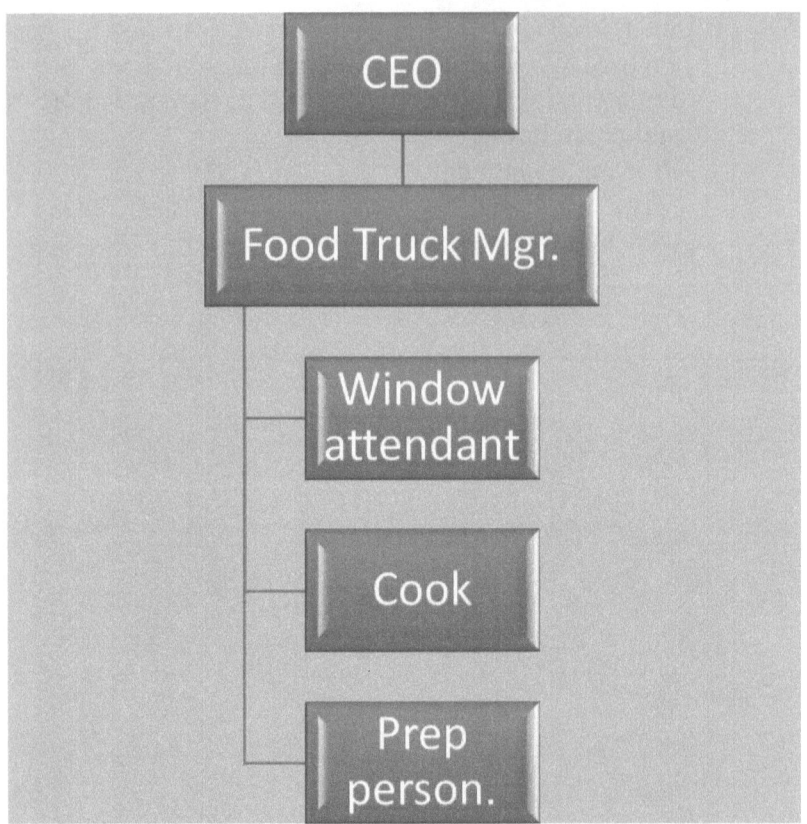

Marketing

Marketing Objectives and Keys to Success

Traditional Marketing

Our first traditional marketing channel will include a (discuss your advertising ideas related to mailers, building signs, etc.).

Internet Marketing

The importance of a professionally designed website cannot be understated. To exploit this opportunity, (Food Truck name) will create and maintain a website with links to our social media channels. The objective of the strategy is to effectively communicate the menu items that we offer.

Social Media Marketing

(Name of the Food Truck)'s social media advertising will include Instagram, Twitter, and Facebook. Using a three-channel approach to social media will ensure our message reaches a broad audience, which will consist of our target market.

Financial Projections

Financial Assumptions

Our financial projections have several assumptions based on research and management's expectation of potential sales and costs.

- All financial projections are based on management and or owner(s) professional expectations of sales and expenses for the foreseeable future.

- In the first 12 months, sales should increase by approximately (percent)% each month. In months 13 to 24, sales growth should slow to approximately (percent)% per month. For years three through five, sales are expected to grow by (percent)%.

- The cost of goods or variable costs are expected to be approximately (percent)% of total sales.

- The initial advertising budget will be $(a dollar amount). Advertising is projected to increase by approximately (percent)% per year. This is to ensure maximum utilization of the firm's assets.

- Cost projections were calculated using a common size model. This practice is typical for financial modeling.

- The tax rate was assumed to be (percent)%. Fluctuation in the tax rate will have a direct impact on net profits.

- The initial funding needed is $(a dollar amount). An increase/decrease in amount will impact the net present value and internal rate of return.

- Starting cash balance needed is $(a dollar amount) for working capital.

- A cash account was used to balance assets with liabilities and equity.

Financial Summary

The financial projections are based on market research and empirical examination of the Food Truck industry. For the next year, we project revenues of approximately $(a dollar amount). The estimated expense costs will be $(a dollar amount). After taxes, we estimate a net profit of $(a dollar amount). This leads to a profit margin of approximately (percent)%. As our brand continues to grow, second-year progression is anticipated to yield a net income of approximately $(a dollar amount). Within five years, net income should exceed $(a dollar amount).

Startup Costs

Startup Costs	
Category	Estimate
Equity Investment	
Loan	
Initial Build Out	
Working Capital	
Section: Equipment	
Sub Total	
Section: Operations	

Sub Total	
Section: Office Equipment	
Sub Total	
Section: Other	
Sub Total	
Total	

Daily Revenues

Average Daily Sales						
Revenue Generators						
Daily Sales	Num.	Price	Cost	Profit	Total Rev.	Total Cost
Section 1						
Item 1						
Item 2						
Item 3						
Section 2						
Item 1						
Item 2						
Item 3						

			Total		

Labor

Labor				
Employee	Number	Rate	Monthly Hours	Total Pay
Salary				
Manager				
Employees				
			Total	

Monthly Fixed Costs

Monthly Fixed Costs	
Monthly Costs	Monthly Total
Rent	
Utilities	
Office Expenses	
Insurance	
Accounting/legal	
Advertising	
Other	
Monthly Total	

Growth Rates

Growth Rates	
Growth Rate Sales 2 & 3	%
Growth Rate Sales 4 & 5	%
Growth Rate Cost of Goods	%
Growth Rate Salary	%
Growth Rate Labor	%

Growth Advertising	%
Growth Office	%
Growth Utility	%
Growth Legal	%
Growth Insurance	%
Growth Other	%

Misc. Information

Misc. Information	
Tax Rate	%
Cost of Capital	%

Loan Payment Calculations

Loan Information	
Loan Amount	
Interest Rate	%
Term	
Payment	

Profit and Loss Quarter 1

Pro Forma Income Statement Year 1 Quarter 1				
	Month 1	Month 2	Month 3	Quarter 1
Revenues				
COGS				
Gross Profit				
Expenses				
Salary				
Labor				
Advertising				
Office				

Expen.				
Rent				
Utilities				
Legal / Account				
Insurance				
Depreciation				
Other				
Total Expenses				
EBIT				
Interest Expense				
EBT				
Taxes				
Net Income				

Profit and Loss Quarter 2

Pro Forma Income Statement Year 1 Quarter 2				
	Month 1	Month 2	Month 3	Quarter 1
Revenues				
COGS				
Gross Profit				
Expenses				
Salary				
Labor				
Advertising				
Office Expen.				
Rent				

Utilities				
Legal / Account				
Insurance				
Depreciation				
Other				
Total Expenses				
EBIT				
Interest Expense				
EBT				
Taxes				
Net Income				

Profit and Loss Quarter 3

Pro Forma Income Statement Year 1 Quarter 3				
	Month 1	Month 2	Month 3	Quarter 1
Revenues				
COGS				
Gross Profit				
Expenses				
Salary				
Labor				
Advertising				
Office Expen.				
Rent				
Utilities				
Legal / Account				

Insurance				
Depreciation				
Other				
Total Expenses				
EBIT				
Interest Expense				
EBT				
Taxes				
Net Income				

Profit and Loss Quarter 4

Pro Forma Income Statement Year 1 Quarter 4				
	Month 1	**Month 2**	**Month 3**	**Quarter 1**
Revenues				
COGS				
Gross Profit				
Expenses				
Salary				
Labor				
Advertising				
Office Expen.				
Rent				
Utilities				
Legal / Account				
Insurance				
Depreciation				

Other				
Total Expenses				
EBIT				
Interest Expense				
EBT				
Taxes				
Net Income				

Income Statement

Pro Forma Income Statement Year 1 Quarter 1				
	Year 1	Year 2	Year 3	Year 4
Revenues				
COGS				
Gross Profit				
Expenses				
Salary				
Labor				
Advertising				
Office Expen.				
Rent				
Utilities				
Legal / Account				
Insurance				
Depreciation				
Other				
Total Expenses				

EBIT				
Interest Expense				
EBT				
Taxes				
Net Income				

Balance Sheet

Balance Sheet - Pro Forma					
Assets	Year 1	Year 2	Year 3	Year 4	Year 5
Cash					
Accts Receiv.					
Invent.					
Total Curr. Assets					
PP&E					
Less Deprec.					
Net PP&E					
Total Assets					

Balance Sheet - Pro Forma					
Liabilities	Year 1	Year 2	Year 3	Year 4	Year 5
Accounts Pay					
Notes Payable					
Accruals					
Total Current					

Liab.					
Loans					
Total Liab.					
Common Stock					
Retained Earnings					
Total Com. Equity					
Total Liab & Equity					

Financial Ratios

Financial Ratios					
	Year 1	Year 2	Year 3	Year 4	Year 5
Return on Equity					
Return on Asset					
Current Ratio					
Profit Margin					
Net Present Value					
IRR					

Funding Request

To start operations, funding of $(a dollar amount) in debt or equity from a bank or investor is required. Debt funding is expected to have a term of (number) to (number) years with an interest rate between (percent)% to (percent)%. Principle and interest payments will be made monthly, using profits from the business. For investors, a negotiated percentage of ownership in the Food Truck will be offered. Also, investors will be compensated through (monthly, quarter, semi-annually) dividend payments from business cash flows.

Received funds will be used as follows:

Startup Costs	
Category	Estimate
Equity Investment	
Loan	
Initial Build Out	
Working Capital	
Section: Equipment	
Sub Total	
Section: Operations	
Sub Total	

Section: Office Equipment	
Sub Total	
Section: Other	
Sub Total	
Total	